"Get ready. Get ready
God's Best-Kept Secre
gator, Mark will lead you on a marvelous journey to discover your
identity in Christ and how to live by grace. Reading this book will
be one of the best decisions you've ever made!"

—**Derwin Gray**, lead pastor of Transformation Church;
author of *Limitless Life*

"It's powerful and refreshing to read a book on grace that's accessible, practical, profound, and life-giving. Because Mark understands the heart of God so honestly and authentically, he is able
to give us challenges and insights that help distill and clarify truth
from the lies we've told ourselves. He's reclaiming for Christians
the life we came to Jesus for: full life, freedom, and heartfelt obedience. This book will free many for years to come."

—**John Lynch**, coauthor of *The Cure*

"This book carries the potential to change your entire outlook on
God and life itself. Prepare to be surprised and encouraged by the
powerful and liberating truths it contains. If you read only one
Christian book this year, let *God's Best-Kept Secret* be the one!"

—**Andrew Farley**, bestselling author of *The Naked Gospel*;
host of *Andrew Farley LIVE* on Sirius XM

"With the heart of a counselor and the mind of a theologian,
Mark Maulding wonderfully unpacks what God has clearly told
us but few of us have grasped: the Christian life is not about our
striving effort but about Christ living in us. Scales will drop from
your eyes as you absorb the liberating truth of the actual good
news and enter into Christ's fullness. I am thrilled about this gift
to the body of Christ!"

—**David Gregory**, *New York Times* bestselling
author of *Dinner with a Perfect Stranger*

"Secrets intrigue us. We want to know what they are. Most of the time they disappoint—but not *God's Best-Kept Secret*. This one will change your life. Mark Maulding has been revealing this secret for years through his counseling and speaking ministry. Now he brings his wealth of experience and keen insights to this wonderful book. Read it carefully and discover all God has for you in Christ Jesus. You will be glad you did!"

—**Bob Christopher**, president of Basic Gospel
and author of *Simple Gospel, Simply Grace*

"On this five-hundredth anniversary of the Reformation, most Christians have yet to discover how to live from their spiritual union with Christ. Mark discerns that the believer's new spirit—rather than the soul—is the basis for their new identity and nature. Although the 'secret' Mark shares seems too good to be true, his use of biblical support, personal testimonies, and practical applications confirm the wisdom of taking the easier yoke of grace discipleship."

—**Dr. John Woodward**, director of counseling and training,
Grace Fellowship International

"Jesus promised to *all* who believe in him the experience of abundant life. Yet sadly, so few Christians seem to attain it. In this wonderful new book, Mark Maulding offers not only an explanation for why but also the way to lay hold of that promised abundant life. I heartily recommend this great new book!"

—**Frank Friedmann**, teaching pastor, Grace Life Fellowship

GOD'S BEST-KEPT
SECRET

God's Best-Kept SECRET

Christianity Is Easier Than You Think

Mark Maulding

BakerBooks
a division of Baker Publishing Group
Grand Rapids, Michigan

© 2017 by Mark Maulding

Published by Baker Books
a division of Baker Publishing Group
PO Box 6287, Grand Rapids, MI 49516-6287
www.bakerbooks.com

Printed in the United States of America

Library of Congress Cataloging-in-Publication Data is on file at the Library of Congress, Washington, DC.

ISBN 978-0-8010-9325-8

Unless otherwise indicated, Scripture quotations are from the Holy Bible, New International Version®. NIV®. Copyright © 1973, 1978, 1984, 2011 by Biblica, Inc.™ Used by permission of Zondervan. All rights reserved worldwide. www.zondervan.com

Scripture quotations labeled GNT are from the Good News Translation—Second Edition. Copyright © 1992 by American Bible Society. Used by permission.

Scripture quotations labeled Message are from THE MESSAGE. Copyright © by Eugene H. Peterson 1993, 1994, 1995, 1996, 2000, 2001, 2002. Used by permission of NavPress. All rights reserved. Represented by Tyndale House Publishers, Inc.

Scripture quotations labeled NASB are from the New American Standard Bible®, copyright © 1960, 1962, 1963, 1968, 1971, 1972, 1973, 1975, 1977, 1995 by The Lockman Foundation. Used by permission. (www.Lockman.org)

Scripture quotations labeled NKJV are from the New King James Version®. Copyright © 1982 by Thomas Nelson, Inc. Used by permission. All rights reserved.

Scripture quotations labeled NLT are from the Holy Bible, New Living Translation, copyright © 1996, 2004, 2015 by Tyndale House Foundation. Used by permission of Tyndale House Publishers, Inc., Carol Stream, Illinois 60188. All rights reserved.

Scripture quotations labeled TLB are from The Living Bible, copyright © 1971. Used by permission of Tyndale House Publishers, Inc., Carol Stream, Illinois 60188. All rights reserved.

Some names and details of the people and situations described in this book have been changed or presented in composite form in order to ensure the privacy of those with whom the author has worked.

17   18   19   20   21   22   23   7   6   5   4   3   2   1

In keeping with biblical principles of creation stewardship, Baker Publishing Group advocates the responsible use of our natural resources. As a member of the Green Press Initiative, our company uses recycled paper when possible. The text paper of this book is composed in part of post-consumer waste.

To Christians everywhere
whom God has been preparing
with great care to discover
his best-kept secret

Contents

1

Secrets Christians Never Share

"I want people to go to heaven, but I don't want them to become a Christian and wind up feeling miserable like me!"

Charlotte whispered this confession as tears streamed down her face. No one would have ever expected that she'd kept this secret to herself for years. Charlotte was married to a lawyer, had four wonderful children, knew the Bible backward and forward, and had a likable personality. Yet by her own admission she had had a mental breakdown because of her Christian beliefs. No matter how hard she tried, Charlotte just couldn't seem to get Christianity to work for her. When I was asked to meet her at a local hospital, she was obviously depressed as well as confused. Charlotte confided to me what she had never told anyone—she was beginning to lose her faith in God.

◇◇◇◇◇◇◇

"Last week, I was reading my Bible and praying. But just five minutes after I finished, I found myself yelling at my husband and kids. What's wrong with me?" Shana spoke these words as she was sitting in my counseling office with a puzzled expression on her face. "How is it possible to be shouting at my family right after I've felt so spiritual?" she asked. "Why do I get angry so quickly?" Shana is not alone. She echoes the same secrets many sincere men and women have revealed to me in private.

◇◇◇◇◇◇◇

Jake came to see me about a destructive habit he was struggling to overcome. He genuinely loved Jesus and was serving in full-time ministry. Yet his own behavior was kicking his butt.

"When I've asked other Christians—even my mentor, a mega-church pastor—how to break this habit, they tell me to pray and read my Bible more. But even though I've dramatically increased the amount of time I pray and read the Bible, it hasn't worked for me. In some ways, I am worse now than before!"

Jake looked at me through eyes filled with despair, anger, and confusion. When I asked him how long he'd been struggling, he hung his head in shame and said, "It's been years."

◇◇◇◇◇◇◇

"I thought if I genuinely tried to obey God, then he wouldn't let anything bad happen to me or my family. Boy, was I wrong."

Geraldo said these words with a furrowed brow. Ever since he'd decided to get serious about obeying God, it seemed as though bad things happened to him more than ever. He didn't get the promotion his boss had promised and his four-year-old daughter had just been diagnosed with a rare disease. Geraldo stared at the floor, wondering why God would let these things happen.

◇◇◇◇◇◇◇

Have you ever kept thoughts to yourself about God, your personal life, or your spiritual life? Have you ever wondered if there might be something better than the kind of relationship you presently have with God? Maybe you've held these kinds of thoughts deep inside:

- *How can I encourage someone else to become a Christian when I don't have my own life figured out?*
- *I've tried following biblical principles to improve my marriage, but we feel closer to a divorce than to each other.*
- *I'm afraid to tell my Christian friends I've fallen into an overwhelming sense of depression. They might judge me or tell me I just need to trust God more.*

As a Christian counselor and speaker for more than twenty years, I've listened to hundreds of Christians tell me their innermost secrets. These individuals include sincere people who've tried to follow inspiring sermons motivating them to live good Christian lives. They've served in their local church, gone on mission trips, and even witnessed to the people around them. Amid all their efforts, however, something still seems to be missing from their faith, and they don't know why. The quiet admissions above are some of the most common ones I've heard. You could call them secrets Christians never share.

Believe me—I understand how Charlotte, Shana, Jake, and Geraldo feel, because I've been there too. At one time in my life I harbored two deep secrets. For a long time, I was obsessed with these thoughts:

Sometimes I wish I weren't a Christian, because non-Christians seem so much happier than me.

If this is all there is to being a Christian, it doesn't work. Something is wrong. I just can't go on living like this.

One night I did share that last thought with my wife as we settled into bed. I blurted that I felt burned out trying to live the Christian life and that I couldn't continue. After waiting patiently for me to share my heart, she responded compassionately. She assured me she truly believed God had an answer that would resolve why I couldn't go on with Christianity as I understood it.

After turning off the lamp, I laid flat on my back, staring at the dark ceiling. I wasn't praying. I wasn't thinking about God. I wasn't thinking about Bible verses. I couldn't do any of that any longer. I was simply thinking about how miserable I was. The room may have been dark, but my soul felt even darker.

How had I gotten here? What had gone wrong? At one time I really enjoyed being a Christian. Over time, though, trying to live the Christian life had become a burden instead of a blessing. Christianity was literally stressing me out!

I wasn't simply tired; I was exhausted. My faith in God was burned out, and I was at the lowest point I'd ever been.

For years I'd been taught that the keys to the Christian life were reading the Bible, praying, hanging around other Christians, going to church, and serving God. I took all that to heart. I even got to the place where I had redoubled my efforts. Instead of praying for a few minutes, I'd try to pray for an hour. Instead of reading one chapter in the Bible, I'd read two or more. Or at least that was my goal, although I often failed. Instead of fasting occasionally, I fasted every week. I figured if these activities were the keys to making the Christian life work, then surely I would break out of my spiritual funk.

The results, though, were just the opposite. I didn't feel any peace or joy or the abundant life Jesus proclaimed. Instead, I had a knot in my stomach from these activities, leaving me feeling drained to the point that I couldn't do any of it.

That's how I ended up harboring secrets that made me feel awful and exhausted. Looking back on that dark night of my soul, sometimes I laugh to myself and think that was when God exclaimed in heaven, "Finally! Mark has stopped trying to hide his secrets and admitted something is wrong. Now I can show him who I really am and what true Christianity really is." God knew I was ready to let go of my secrets and see a new perspective based on the truth of who he is. I wasn't giving up on God or Christianity. I was simply giving up on God and Christianity as I knew it.

Is your view of God and Christianity working for you? Like many other Christians, do you harbor a secret inside? Have you ever slowed down long enough to ask what you really think about God, deep down in your soul?

These secrets all have their foundation in an incorrect view of God and inaccurate expectations of him and ourselves. First you'll figure out how you view God by taking this quiz and doing a few revealing exercises. Then we'll explore some other factors that may have affected your view of God, such as your family and religion.

The God Is Quiz

What do you really believe about God? Is he who you think he is? To consider these questions, take the God Is Quiz. Read each of the twenty statements below and answer "true" or "false" beside each statement. Don't overthink your answers. And don't give the answer you think you're supposed to give, such as the Sunday-school, in-front-of-people answer. Go with your first response.

True or False:

1. I worship God because he is a holy God. _____
2. I enjoy God because he is a loving Father. _____
3. I am often aware of God's presence in me. _____
4. I know God loves me no matter what happens. _____
5. God is proud of me just because I am his child. _____
6. I obey God because he loves me, not so he'll love me more. _____

7. I feel unconditionally accepted by God. _____

8. I feel very comfortable calling God "Dad" or "Papa." _____

9. God is more interested in me than in what I do for him. _____

10. God never gets angry with me. _____

11. God must love me because many blessings happen to me. _____

12. I am afraid of God's punishment when I sin. _____

13. I feel as though I can never please God. _____

14. Making my life work seems mostly up to me instead of up to God. _____

15. I believe I must do the right things to get closer to God. _____

16. I feel as though God is often disappointed with me. _____

17. God seems good when good things happen to me. _____

18. I need to put myself in the right position for God to bless me. _____

19. God doesn't really show up when I need him. _____

20. Based on what he lets happen to me, God seems mad at me. _____

Your answers to these twenty statements reflect your personal view of God. How can you know?

If you answered the first ten questions as true and the last ten questions as false, then you have an accurate view of who God is based on what the Bible really says. If you answered the opposite way, then your view of God may need reconsidering. But here's the good news: that's why I wrote this book.

Let's go a step further in our perception of who God is. For example, wouldn't you agree it's easy to believe God is wonderful when you're enjoying a good day? But what's your view of God on a bad day? And I'm talking about a really awful, heartbreaking type of day. That's when you find out what you truly believe about God.

The God You Really Believe Is the One You View on Your Worst Days

When your life is going well, it's easy to believe God loves you. It's great to proclaim he's good when you ask him to give you something and he does. But life doesn't always go well, does it? What do you feel God is like when he doesn't seem to answer your prayer? How do you feel about him when your circumstances get worse, not better?

When my wife and I had our third child, the doctor came in and said, "Mr. and Mrs. Maulding, you have a baby girl and she seems healthy." But she went on to tell us our daughter had been born with a genetic defect that would cause her to live developmentally disabled for the rest of her life. That was one of my worst days ever. My wife and I cried bitterly, because we had lost the dream of a perfectly healthy child every parent wants. A few years before our daughter's birth, my view of God in that situation would have made me think he was punishing me. I would have wondered what sin I had committed to cause God to hurt me, my wife, and our baby.

What have you thought about God on your worst day?

I know it's not easy, but let's find out—because making this important distinction in your mind is crucial. Think about a really bad day you had. Maybe it was the worst day in your life. You found out you had cancer. The divorce your spouse wanted was final. You were in a debilitating car accident. Your child was hospitalized and you weren't certain she would make it. A close family member died. You had a flat tire and you were late for the new job you just started. You got fired. You were sexually abused. Your best friend betrayed you. You realized you were in such financial debt that you didn't think you would ever get out. You were harassed because of your ethnicity. Your church looked like it was going to split. You were falsely accused publicly.

You fill in the blank.

Then go back in your mind and remember the raw emotions you felt. Do you feel them now? I know it's depressing to recall these memories, but here's the important point: During that difficult time, what did you feel about God and his relationship with you? Was he even in the mix?

Don't try to avoid those memories by believing you shouldn't think about God this way. It's okay. God prefers honesty and truth versus sweeping secrets under the rug. Take a minute or two to recall your view of God on your worst day, what you would have said or did say to him.

What I've heard from people has varied from person to person, but here are some examples:

- God, if you really love me, why are you letting this happen?
- God, I'm not sure if you are even real. Maybe you're just a fairy tale.
- God, I'm mad at you and I don't want to talk to you.
- God, I wonder what I've done for you to do this to me.
- God, I don't believe in you anymore because of what you let happen to me.
- God, it seems as though you have abandoned me.
- God, you love me no matter what is happening.
- God, you are good even if I can't see it right now.
- God, you are sovereign in my life and in control, so I trust you.
- God, you are faithful always, so I can trust you with anything.

You may have had one of these or similar thoughts. But whatever it was, it defined what you truly believed about God, what you really thought about him.

Your view of God, however, goes beyond the way you feel on your worst day. We can get an even better picture when we consider God and ourselves together in relationship. Do these exercises to reveal how you feel about God, because how we *feel* shows us what we really believe.

Exercise #1: God through the Lens of a Selfie

Many people find it fun to take pictures of themselves or close-up photos with family and friends called "selfies." But what if you could take a selfie with God? What would your picture look like if you could take a photo of you and God together?

You might think your selfie with God will look different depending on the situation. So once again take a minute to think back to one of your worst days. Then imagine taking a selfie with God in that situation. What would your picture look like? Think about this image.

At one time in my life, my selfie with God would have showed him sternly pointing to the next thing he wanted me to do. I'd be in the picture, but I'd be standing a few feet away, looking half-eager and half-tired, trying to obey.

When I've asked people to describe their selfie with God, here are some images they've described. Which mental picture do you relate to the most?

- God is not in the picture. I am standing there alone.
- God is far back in the background, far away from me.
- God is on his throne. I see steps between us, but they are broken.
- God has a stick in his hand, and I have a terrible look of fear on my face as I wait for him to punish me for a sin I just committed.
- God has his arms folded and a frustrated look on his face that says, "Why can't you get it together?"

19

- God looks disappointed as both he and I are nervously looking down at the ground beside each other.
- God has his arm around me and I have my arm around him.
- God is on his throne and tears are running down my face as I kneel and worship him.
- God is giving me a big hug, and I'm hugging him back.
- God is mad at me, and I'm crying because I always mess up.
- God is faceless, and I'm emotionless.

Do you relate to one or more of those selfies? Keep that picture in mind as we see how your view of God may be shaped more by your family than you think.

Exercise #2: God through the Lens of Family

One of the challenges you may have is that your view of God was shaped more by your family than what you read in the Bible. My counseling staff and I see this problem on a regular basis when we help people understand their actual concept of God. When we go over the history of their lives, they sometimes see how their relationship with their earthly father has influenced their view of God.

It was certainly true for me. Let me describe how my relationship with my dad related to how I once saw God. (My dad and I have talked about this, and I have received his permission to share this information.)

My dad would have given his life for me. There is no doubt that he loved me then and loves me now. He provided for me and our family. He came to my basketball games in high school and was there for other important events.

Yet when he asked me to do some kind of project, he had a habit of coming behind me, redoing it, or telling me what I did wrong more than what I did right. As an adult, I talked to him about this and he apologized, not realizing he was doing it. But this is what was happening as I grew up.

For example, we had a fairly large yard that was hilly and full of pine trees. We lived where it was hot and humid, and we had a push mower to cut the grass. As you can imagine, it was hard work.

I started mowing our yard when I was around fourteen years old, and I could never finish it in one day. Finally, toward the end of the summer when I was fifteen, for the first time I mowed the entire yard in one day. I was so excited I had accomplished this feat. I couldn't wait for my dad to get home from work so I could tell him.

I sat on the front steps of our home, anticipating what it was going to be like when he drove up. When he pulled into the garage, I rushed over to his car door. As he stepped out, I shouted, "Dad, I mowed the lawn and finished the whole yard all in one day!"

Dad stepped out to the front lawn, inspected it, and then said only one thing: "You missed a spot." I was crushed. This imprinted on me that I couldn't fully please my dad. It felt like no matter what I did for him, it was never quite good enough.

I didn't know it at the time, but these types of comments from my dad definitely shaped how I viewed my heavenly Father. When I became serious about my relationship with God, I really wanted him to be proud of me as well. I worked hard to obey and serve him. Yet deep down, I felt as though I could never fully please him either. It often felt like he was coming behind me, saying, "You missed a spot."

Our view of God, however, is not always negatively influenced by our families. For example, my wife's father was loving, affectionate, and kind. She had a great relationship with him and felt loved, accepted, and important. His love was unconditional and she didn't feel as though she had anything to prove. But she wanted to obey him just because she knew how much he loved her.

That is how she has always seen her heavenly Father—loving, kind, and accepting of her. She's wanted to obey him just because she knew how much he loved her. Over the years, God has grown her understanding of who he is, and she had a good model in her dad.

When you think about your relationship with God, do you see any parallels with your family? Your perspective could have been influenced by your dad, or it could have been affected by your relationship with your mom, a grandparent, an uncle, or even someone outside your family, such as a pastor or priest.

Keep in mind, though, not only our families influence our view of God. Another big contributing factor is religion itself.

Exercise #3: God through the Lens of Religion

Would it surprise you if I said God is not religious? Do you think he is? Would you describe God as someone who is mostly interested in giving people rules to live by? Would you define a relationship with God as being blessed when you obey and punished when you disobey? In other words, do you believe God is religious in that he is all about rule-keeping? What does the Bible actually say on this topic?

Let's start with Genesis, the first book of the Bible, where we see God's purpose in creating mankind. Genesis 2:7 explains who God is and his motivations: "Then the LORD God formed a man out of dust from the ground and breathed into his nostrils the breath of life, and man became a living being."

As we dig into this verse, we see that it reveals a fantastic love story between God and mankind. Use your imagination for a moment and become that first man. Your gender doesn't matter; just pretend you are Adam when God created him.

Visualize how God has just taken dirt from the ground and formed every cell of your body into a perfect being. Your skin, your eyes, your ears, your hair, your arms, your legs, your face are all perfect. He is looking you over, admiring his creation. But you aren't fully human yet. You're lying there motionless. One more ingredient is needed to make you a real person.

God leans over your lifeless body and gently blows the "breath of life" into your nostrils.

The word *breath* here doesn't mean "oxygen" but "spirit." It means God blew the Holy Spirit into you as he was creating your human spirit. And the word *life* means "lives," plural. This seems to be a clear reference to the entire Trinity entering you to live in you. As they do, you come alive and begin to breathe. Then you open your eyes, and the first thing you see is God looking at you with love.

The last part of Genesis 2:7 says you became a living being. The word *being* means "soul," which is your mind, emotions, and will. Your soul has also come alive. With God living in you, only now are you fully human. You are the person he had in mind long before he created you. You are the human prototype for every human to be born after you. A human was originally designed to live in a relationship with God by God indwelling him or her. That is what makes us fully human.

What do you learn about God from this verse? You learn he is your Creator. You were his idea. You exist because he wanted you to be here. That immediately gives you a great sense of value. You also realize God has intended to unite himself with you from the beginning of time. He wanted to be your source of life. He wanted to be close to you. Why? Because the God who is love created you to live loved in the depths of your being.

Let me put it this way: God brought you into this world because he wanted to live in union with you. He wanted to have intimacy with you. Maybe you've heard intimacy means "Into me you see." This means he wanted to enjoy you, and he wanted you to enjoy him.

God did not create you because he needed someone to love him. The Father, Son, and Holy Spirit have been fully satisfied with the love and intimacy they shared together long before you and I came along. But if he didn't need us, then why did he create us?

I hope the answer I am about to share with you blows your mind and removes any sense that God is religious.

God was so full of love that he wanted to share it with another creature with whom he could unite himself. He wanted to share himself with you! You've been invited into the fellowship of the Trinity!

This is why humankind began. This is what God is like. Just as with Adam, God created you to have a relationship with him and to live with purpose. In Adam's case, God knew he would enjoy naming the animals and taking care of the garden of Eden. Then, after all that was started, God gave Adam only one rule, in Genesis 2:16–17:

> And the LORD God commanded the man, "You are free to eat from any tree in the garden; but you must not eat from the tree of the knowledge of good and evil, for when you eat from it you will certainly die."

Consider the importance of these verses and put yourself in Adam's place. God didn't create you and then give you a bunch of religious rules to force you to worship him and love him. God gave you himself and only one rule that was intended for your good. If God were religious by nature, then he would have written down the Ten Commandments immediately and given them to everyone. But you didn't need them because his desire from the beginning was to live in you! He wanted to be your life source and to love you from within.

Do you see now that God is not religious? We'll discuss the purpose of the Ten Commandments later in this book, but it will all relate back to our beginning days before sin entered the world.

Of course, Adam and Eve blew it for all of us when they ate from that tree. Their sin was passed on to us when we were born.

But God's intent has been to live inside of every human being who came after Adam and Eve. Even better, in the midst of our sin, God loved you and me so much that he sent his Son, Jesus Christ, for two reasons.

First, so Jesus could be exalted before all creation. Second, so God could live in you, which he has always wanted to do. His plan to live within you has never changed. He has always wanted to love you and for you to love him. Contrary to what you may have heard or felt, you can't make God stop loving you, because he is not religious.

Let's Blow the Lid Off God's Best-Kept Secret

Looking back to my dark days when I felt miserable as a Christian, I mistakenly believed God was religious, angry, distant, unloving, and impossible to please. No wonder I was a wreck. My mistaken view of God led me to experience depression, bondage to lustful habits, discouragement, and physical pain.

Did I mention I was a church pastor at the time?

Thankfully, God began to show me the best-kept secret in Christianity. God revealed the gospel as he wants all Christians to understand it. He began replacing my stinking thinking with the truth of who he really is. Little by little, I was able to let go of my mistaken beliefs. God took me from relating to him as stoically religious to enjoying an intimacy with him I still have difficulty putting into words today.

To say I was transformed is an understatement. When God exchanged my warped view of him for the true view of him, he changed me from the inside out. My depression was exchanged for joy. My discouragement was exchanged for hope. My continual battle with many sinful habits was exchanged for victory, without my even trying. Much more happened that I will share later in this book.

You might think my story sounds too good to be true. But the transforming power of God is real. Sadly, so many Christians live without knowing how God really is. They also don't know how he views them. It's almost as if the reality of God's amazing life and deep love within us remains a secret. You could call it God's best-kept secret because so few seem to know the truth. But I don't mean God is keeping it a secret. He is not! God wants everyone to experience life as he intended.

God's best-kept secret is this: the Christian life is easier than you think because you already have everything you need in Christ to live it! This is revealed in the New Covenant, which this book will unpack one truth at a time.

I've given my life to teaching this great message of freedom to anyone who will listen. As I have shared it around the world, the typical response I get is, "Why haven't I heard this before?" To some Christians, this message seems like something buried in the Bible, yet it's been right under their noses the whole time. Well, I think it's time to blow the lid off it!

Are you ready to learn more about God's best-kept secret?

2

Christians Don't Need to Focus on Right and Wrong

Here I was again at my secret hiding place. I had slipped away to a remote field to sit on a large stump. I wanted to be alone to think about why I was unsuccessful as a pastor. I was in the third year of founding a new church, and it wasn't growing as I had hoped. I saw this as a reflection on me and my self-worth.

I often had lunch with another pastor named Jessie, who was also starting a new church. I told him how discouraged I felt with the lack of growth in the congregation. Rather than responding directly, he would talk about how we could be more spiritual or what we could "do" for our churches. He wasn't a bad guy. He simply had no answer for me.

I couldn't see then that I equated my expectation of God's blessing of church growth with the number of spiritual activities I performed. All I knew was that I was growing tired and feeling more and more like a failure. I didn't realize it at the time, but I was entering into a place of spiritual burnout.

Many Christians experience spiritual burnout, but few are willing to admit it. It's the perfect way to describe how I felt that day at the age of thirty. I was mentally tired. I was emotionally tired. I was physically tired. Most of all, I was tired of Christianity.

But here's what I didn't see coming. My burnout eventually led me to a startling discovery. All my efforts to gain self-worth and self-acceptance by living like a super-Christian were not from God. They were Satan's perversion of Christianity, which I like to call "Checklist Christianity." I had been deceived by it!

Checklist Christianity is the false belief that God wants us to focus on doing what is right and avoiding what is wrong. As a result, we believe he has a long checklist of all the right things he expects us to complete each day. It's easy to fall into this trap. Since we want God to bless us, we take a daily inventory of our mental list and check off what we've done. If we have done most of the items, then it is a good day and we believe our efforts will result in blessings from God. But if we haven't done enough on the checklist, we will have a bad day and God will be disappointed. We fear a lack of blessings or that punishment awaits us.

When you consider this ridiculous system, no wonder so many Christians burn out. Who can keep up such a crazy checklist that consistently? If you are motivated in your relationship with God by obligation, fear, and guilt, you will eventually hit a wall.

The good news is God was there when I hit the wall. Sometimes I wish I had known the truth of the New Covenant then so I wouldn't have had to go through what I did. But if I hadn't, I probably wouldn't have such compassion for those who experience it in their own lives. I also wouldn't have had the passion to share God's best-kept secret with thousands of Christians.

Checklist Christianity Comes from Living in the Wrong Tree

The phenomenon of Checklist Christianity is not new. Way back in the garden of Eden, we find two very important trees: the Tree of Life and the Tree of the Knowledge of Good and Evil. Genesis 2:9 says,

> The LORD God made all kinds of trees grow out of the ground—trees that were pleasing to the eye and good for food. In the middle of the garden were the tree of life and the tree of the knowledge of good and evil.

Both trees were real trees, but they represented how Adam and Eve were going to choose to live. The Tree of Life represented how God wanted every human to live—dependent on the life of Christ within them. The Tree of the Knowledge of Good and Evil represented living independent of God. The couple chose poorly.

> When the woman saw that the fruit of the tree was good for food and pleasing to the eye, and also desirable for gaining wisdom, she took some and ate it. She also gave some to her husband, who was with her, and he ate it. (Gen. 3:6)

The moment Adam and Eve ate from this tree their thinking changed from a relationship mentality to a checklist mentality. Their list was about what is good and evil, right and wrong. This was fake godliness. It was replacing godliness with human good and evil, right and wrong. Before this, everything they did was motivated by the belief that God loved them and had blessed them. Now they believed if they performed well and could check off more right than wrong each day, God would love and bless them. But if they committed more wrong than right, God would reject and punish them. This is when religion began.

We see this illustrated immediately when God came looking for them in the cool of the day. Adam and Eve hid from God because they were afraid of him. It had never entered their minds to be afraid of him before they ate from that tree. They had only felt love for God.

> Then the man and his wife heard the sound of the LORD God as he was walking in the garden in the cool of the day, and they hid from the LORD God among the trees of the garden. (v. 8)

Sin, by its very nature, perverts a person's thinking to be upside down about God, ourselves, and other people. That's why God says in Isaiah 55:8–9,

> "My thoughts are not your thoughts, neither are your ways my ways," declares the LORD. "As the heavens are higher than the earth, so are my ways higher than your ways and my thoughts than your thoughts."

Unfortunately, we all inherited that same thinking from Adam and Eve, and it doesn't automatically go away once we become Christians. That's why it's so easy to make Christianity about right and wrong, turning it into a checklist, something God doesn't care about at all!

Sadly, a lot of Christian teaching and discipleship fosters Checklist Christianity, using the Bible to focus on doing right instead of wrong. This is simply swinging from the evil side to the good side of that tree. It's where the false idea of being a good Christian comes from. God wants us to enjoy the fruit of the Tree of Life by living dependent on the life of Christ in us.

Let me be clear. *God isn't interested in right and wrong. What he is interested in is life—you and me living from his life within us!*

Jesus Restarted the Human Race

God created Adam with the intent of living in and through him. When he fashioned Eve from Adam's rib, she instantly had God

30

in her too. God's original plan for every person born after Adam and Eve was that he would live in and through them. Once Adam sinned, though, God would not live in anyone. Because he is holy, he will not coexist with sin, and we are all born sinners. When Jesus Christ came, he "restarted" the human race and made it possible for God to come live in people again.

Did you know Jesus Christ was called the last Adam when he came to this earth? First Corinthians 15:45 says, "So also it is written, 'The first man, Adam, became a living soul.' The last Adam became a life-giving spirit" (NASB). Jesus was called the last Adam because he came to restart the human race. Here's what that means.

Jesus Christ came to this earth 100 percent God and 100 percent human. Would you be surprised, though, if I told you he never once relied on his deity to live his life, to do ministry or miracles? Although he never stopped being God, he lived only as a human. That is why Philippians 2:6–7 says of him,

> Who, although He existed in the form of God, did not regard equality with God a thing to be grasped, but emptied Himself, taking the form of a bond-servant, and being made in the likeness of men. (NASB)

Jesus Christ did everything he did as a human by completely relying on his Father to live in and through him, just as Adam was supposed to have done. As he did, he lived a perfect life of love. This includes all his obedience and his ministry. He said so himself in Scriptures such as John 14:10–11:

> Do you not believe that I am in the Father, and the Father is in Me? The words that I say to you I do not speak on My own initiative, but the Father abiding in Me does His works. Believe Me that I am in the Father and the Father is in Me; otherwise believe because of the works themselves. (NASB)

31

Jesus came to restore what Adam had lost. He lived as Adam was to have lived—dependent on God in him to live through him. And just as everyone born after Adam was to have had God in them, Jesus made a way through his death, burial, and resurrection for God to reenter every human who would be born again. That is why we read earlier in 1 Corinthians 15:45 that Jesus Christ, the last Adam, was a "life-giving" spirit, giving the life of God back to everyone who believes in him for salvation.

We may believe we are supposed to use the behavior of Jesus as our example so we can live as he did in some kind of checklist way, but nothing could be further from the truth. But God has come to live in us because we are to live dependent on him in us to live through us—just as Jesus did. That is how you can truly live like Jesus.

No Checklist for You to Accomplish in Life Exists

One of the key characteristics of living by checklists as a Christian is that success is supposedly linked to how hard you try. That is why many Christians are addicted to THC, not the chemical in marijuana but another THC—Try Harder Christianity. The idea is that if you will just try hard enough to keep your checklist of right and wrong, you will finally live victoriously as a Christian. But if you are failing, you just aren't trying hard enough. Commitment, rededication, putting yourself in a position to be blessed, following hard after Jesus, and paying the price all involve this same Try Harder Christianity idea but never work for long.

God's best-kept secret and only alternative to Checklist Christianity is to exchange it for another THC—Trust Him Christianity, as found in the New Covenant. In each chapter of this book, I will unfold this truth more and more. But for now, let me share the basics of the New Covenant. Through Jesus Christ's death, burial, and resurrection, God has done *for you* and *to you* what you could not do for yourself.

- He has completely forgiven you. You can stop trying hard to get forgiveness. You already have all you will ever need.
- He has given you a new identity. You can stop trying hard to create an identity. He has already given you a great identity—the best you could ever wish for.
- He has come to live in you to love you and live through you. You can stop trying hard to make yourself live a better Christian life. He has already provided his Son, Jesus Christ, in you to do that for you.

Since all of that is true, wouldn't it be freeing to get rid of your checklist? No more thinking,

- *I must read my Bible today—check.*
- *I must pray today—check.*
- *I must give money at church today—check.*
- *I must serve God this week—check.*
- *I must avoid that habitual sin—check.*

These acts are definitely important. But if doing them as a checklist is your main focus, they can produce surprising, unwanted problems, including

- Emotional struggles, such as discouragement, anger, and depression
- Physical problems, such as fatigue and fitful sleep
- Relationship problems, such as conflict in relationships
- Spiritual problems, such as disillusionment, self-condemnation, and rebellion against God

God wants our behavior to be based on the overflow of a dependent, love relationship with Jesus in us, not on trying harder and harder to perform all the tasks on our checklists.

What Do You Do with Your To-Do's?

Recently I spoke to a group of pastors and ministry leaders in Central America, and I met a missionary couple, Marcos and Christina. They were questioning their desire to continue ministry work.

Marcos and Christina had lived Checklist Christianity for many years. They got up early for an hour of prayer and Bible reading. They never missed the weekly prayer meeting with coworkers. They each memorized a verse of Scripture every week. They set aside prayer time each day as a family. They always gave a tithe of their income. They fasted every Friday. Each attempted to lead at least one person to Christ a week. They even had a to-do list for their marriage, which included an obligatory "I love you" each morning.

Yet all this activity failed to produce an intimate relationship with Jesus. It did not give them calm and peace within. Instead they felt far away from God. They began to harbor tremendous anger and resentment with no idea why. Talking with each other always seemed to end in an argument. In reality they just didn't like each other or mission work and didn't want to be around the people they were trying to influence! Marcos and Christina were hanging together by a tiny thread.

Then they heard me teach on Christ living within us, and God gave Marcos a revelation that Jesus Christ was in him not just to save him but to love him and to live through him. In newfound freedom, he started walking around the campus, saying out loud, "Christ is in me to love me and to live through me. Christ is in me to love me and to live through me . . ."

A day later, Christina experienced the same revelation. We met for meals, and I listened to Marcos and Christina describe how their anger and exhaustion began to dissipate. They began to feel a real love for each other and a passion for their calling. As they each relied on Christ in them, his love created a vision to reach others in Central America with newfound hope and energy. They abandoned Checklist Christianity and exchanged it for a beautiful relationship with Christ in them. They got it!

I've counseled Christians, much like Marcos and Christina, who struggle with all kinds of issues, from depression to habitual sins to marital problems. Inevitably, many will reveal their belief in Checklist Christianity when they say in frustration, "Just tell me what to do!"

Too many Christians falsely believe if you just give them a checklist of things to do, they will be able to go home and work on the list. The idea is, "If I can work on my list hard enough, long enough, and pray about it, I can change."

This thinking has two major fallacies. First, if you *can* change yourself this way, you have merely strengthened what the Bible calls the "flesh." The flesh in simple terms is the ways we all live independent of God, but I will define it in greater detail later. God does not want us to strengthen the flesh, but rather to live dependent on him who is our Strength. Second, when people change themselves through their own self-effort, the change doesn't last very long.

God wants you to change, but he wants to change you from the inside out, which only Jesus living in and through you can bring about as you rely on him. In Galatians 2:20 Paul wrote, "I have been crucified with Christ and I no longer live, but Christ lives in me. The life I now live in the body, I live by faith in the Son of God, who loved me and gave himself for me."

This Scripture befuddled me for years. As God gave me a true understanding about the New Covenant, I finally saw it: Jesus Christ was already in me so I could rely on him to live through me. I didn't need a checklist I thought made me a great Christian. I had something amazingly better—him in me! He alone could live through me to make me the best Christian God wanted me to be.

The Christian Life Is Impossible and Easy at the Same Time

If you feel exhausted living the Christian life but are puzzled as to why, the words of Jesus in Matthew 11:28–30 will be music to your ears.

> Come to me, all you who are weary and burdened, and I will give you rest. Take my yoke upon you and learn from me, for I am gentle and humble in heart, and you will find rest for your souls. For my yoke is easy and my burden is light.

In one sense, the Christian life is impossible in that no matter how hard we try, we cannot do it ourselves. If you don't believe that, just hang around any of your family who is challenging to be with for a while. That alone will convince you.

In another sense, though, the Christian life is easy. Jesus said his yoke is easy. A yoke was placed on a horse or ox so that it could pull a heavy load. The yoke, in fact, placed a very heavy load on the animal, which eventually exhausted it. But Jesus is sufficient for us, for when we rely on him, his yoke is easy. The yoke of Jesus is the yoke of grace, not the yoke of the law, trying harder, self-effort, or self-help. He is the yoke!

That doesn't mean life is easy or that we will never feel stress. What it does mean, though, is that through all of life's challenges, we will know where to go for help. We will go to that place of depending on, knowing, and relying on Jesus Christ in us.

Let the Best Person Live through You for Victory

You may not be a sports fan, but allow me to use a sports metaphor to explain the concept of relying upon Christ. Let's say you decide to release some stress by playing basketball. At first you're shooting by yourself in a gym. Soon after, someone walks in and joins you. He asks, "Do you mind if I play basketball with you?"

"That's fine," you reply.

After a while, the other guy asks if you'd like to play a one-on-one game against each other. You agree, but then suddenly realize the other guy is the top college basketball player in America! You know you are probably going to lose, but you don't want to miss the opportunity to play with such a great player.

As the game begins, you find yourself losing—badly. The top college player scores every time and you have no way of stopping him. And when you attempt to score, nothing happens, because you don't have the necessary ability or skills. The final score of the first game is 10 to 0. You get skunked.

Feeling tired and thirsty, you take a break to get some water. As you're bent over the water fountain, you hear a voice behind you saying, "I see you're getting terribly beaten by that college player. Would you like some help to win the next game?"

As you turn around, you find yourself face-to-face with the best player in the NBA. You respond, "Sure! Knowing who you are gives me great hope that I can improve. Just tell me what to do, and I will try really hard to do it."

Then the best NBA player says, "I can tell you what to do, but that will not help you very much. I can offer you something much better. I've figured out a way to step into a person's body and play basketball through them. But there's one catch. If you ask me to come in, you will need to let go of everything you know about playing basketball. Then you will need to depend completely on me to play basketball through you. Are you willing to do this? Are you willing to exchange trust in yourself for complete trust in me?"

You think about this for a moment, because it's a big decision. Finally you say, "Absolutely. I invite you in, and I will rely on you instead of me."

When you go back out to play the next game against the top college player, you get the ball first. You think to yourself, "This feels really awkward to rely on this other person in me. I'm just going to play the way I know how to play." Immediately you find yourself losing badly again. The problem is you still think you know how to play basketball.

Even while you're playing, you hear the voice of the NBA player inside you saying, "Trust me. Listen to me. Let me play through you with my abilities, my skills, and my way of thinking." Slowly but surely, you begin to do just that. You exchange your trust in yourself for trust in the NBA player. Then something amazing happens—you start to score! You're also able to prevent the college player from scoring on you. As you continue to rely on the NBA player, you end up winning the game!

The college player invites you to play again. You excitedly agree. You've discovered that when you rely on the best NBA player to play basketball through you, you win. When you fall back into the old habits of relying on yourself, you lose.

If we apply this metaphor to Galatians 2:20, which you read earlier in this chapter, it would sound like this: "I'm no longer on my own to play basketball. The best NBA player is playing through me. The games I now play, I play by relying on the best NBA player in me."

I don't mean to be trite with this metaphor, and you can apply this to music, video games, and so on. But do you see the connection? Jesus Christ has stepped into your life to play the game of life through you every day. It may be awkward when you first begin to trust him, but over time you will learn to rely more on him and less on yourself.

You might skeptically ask, "Does this mean Christians should ignore training, education, life experiences, and help from other people?" No, not at all. You give those options to Jesus and tell him, "As you live through me, if you want to use any of these, please do. If you don't use them, I trust you completely to live through me anyway."

Does that mean everything you do will turn out great? No. But it does mean that regardless of the outcome, God is pleased when you trust his Son to live life through you.

Take the 7-Day No-Checklist Challenge

If you are ready to stop feeling exhausted living the Christian life, I invite you to take the 7-Day No-Checklist Challenge. Here's how it works:

First, write down all the checklist items you have been following. In other words, what "right" activities have you been doing to try to make the Christian life work for you? For example, do you have a checklist of spiritual disciplines? Do you have a checklist for trying to build certain character traits in your life? Do you have a checklist for all the sins you're not going to think about today? Maybe you have a checklist for how you want to treat your family or friends.

After you identify your Christian Checklist, do something that may feel a little scary, but I'm confident it's what your heavenly Father wants you to do. Light the paper on fire and burn it up. God will not be angry with you for doing so.

You will still desire to do some of the things on your checklist, such as prayer and reading your Bible. Just don't have a checklist for these items or any other spiritual activities. How do you know when your life is no longer governed by a checklist? When you no longer feel guilty for not doing specific activities.

Next, ask God over the next seven days to help you avoid returning to your checklist. Just ask Jesus to live in you and through you each day instead. Why seven days? As you rely on Christ throughout an entire week, my prayer is the Holy Spirit will reveal *to* you Christ *in* you more and more. My desire is that your freedom will continue after the first seven days for the rest of your life!

One evening I was sitting at a coffee shop in Louisiana, where I was speaking at a church, when suddenly a man was standing right in front of me, smiling. He introduced himself as James and began to share that he had heard me preach at that same church several months earlier. He explained that he and his wife have a hard life.

Their daughter has two intellectual disabilities that are stressful to manage. They were always worn-out from taking care of her along with working their day jobs and raising two young sons.

Then James got excited as he said, "Mark, do you remember when you gave everyone a seven-day challenge to let go of their checklist and ask Christ to live through them that first time you preached at our church? Well, I took that challenge. When I went to work, when I was at home, when I was with my wife, when I took care of my disabled daughter—whatever I was doing—I relied on Christ in me. It's made all the difference in the world! I don't get as frustrated and angry as before. I'm much calmer, more patient, and more loving. Thank you for challenging us to ask Christ to live through us. My life has been completely changed. I am forever grateful."

The 7-Day No-Checklist Challenge Prayer

Dear heavenly Father, I admit that I have tried hard to live as a Christian, to keep my checklist of right and wrong for way too long. I'm ready to begin depending on Jesus Christ to live in and through me instead. Literally or in my mind, I take my checklist and burn it into ashes. Now that it is gone, Jesus, I ask you to live in and through me for the next seven days. Holy Spirit, please remind me not to go back to my checklist but to rely on Jesus instead. I pray this is the beginning of how I will live the Christian life for the remainder of my life. By your grace, Amen.

Once you've prayed this prayer of faith, you may have some legitimate questions, such as:

- "How will I know if Jesus is living through me?" Believe by faith that he is, whether or not you feel him—unless God shows you that you are sinning.

- "What if life seems to get harder when I ask him to live through me?" Don't stop asking. This may be spiritual resistance from Satan attempting to get you to give up.
- "What will be the results of Jesus Christ living through me?" In time, the evidence will be the fruit of the Spirit. It will also be the power of the Spirit enabling you to obey more and to serve with greater fruitfulness.

Remember this aspect of God's best-kept secret: no exhausting checklist of right and wrong exists in the Christian life! You have Jesus Christ living within you instead!

3

Christians Believe Weird Stuff about Themselves

Can a Christian be a liar?

Can a Christian be a thief?

Can a Christian be an alcoholic?

Can a Christian be a drug addict?

Can a Christian be a homosexual?

Can a Christian be a sinner?

These are tough questions, but your answers reveal what you believe about God, the gospel, and your view of yourself. It may surprise you that the answer to each question is "no." As a Christian, you cannot be a liar, thief, alcoholic, drug addict, homosexual, sinner, and so on. That doesn't mean Christians don't lie, steal, get drunk, or sin. My point is that God does not define you by your behavior.

Look carefully with me at this change of identity 1 Corinthians 6:9–11 states so beautifully for every Christian. (The bracketed insertions are mine to help define the preceding words.)

Do you not know that wrongdoers will not inherit the kingdom of God? Do not be deceived: Neither the sexually immoral nor idolaters nor adulterers nor men who have sex with men nor thieves nor the greedy nor drunkards nor slanderers nor swindlers will inherit the kingdom of God. And that is what some of you were. But you were washed [forgiven], you were sanctified [made holy], you were justified [made righteous] in the name of the Lord Jesus Christ and by the Spirit of our God.

Did you notice the amazing shift in identity from who we once were in Adam to who we are now in Christ by the phrase "And that is what some of you were"?

This truth reveals one aspect of the best-kept secret about being a Christian: God does not determine who you are by what you do; he determines who you are according to your "birth." I know this idea may seem a little confusing at first, and I'll explain what I mean by the word *birth*. But let's look at the Bible to explore this wonderful reality and apply it to your circumstances. I know it has the power to change your life, because I've seen it happen over and over to thousands of Christians!

Your Original Identity Was Stolen

Have you ever experienced identity theft? It's one of the most common and frustrating crimes in the world today. Yet identity theft isn't a modern issue. The problem goes all the way back to the beginning of human history. In the first part of the Bible, Genesis 1:26 says, "Then God said, 'Let Us make man in Our image, according to Our likeness'" (NASB).

When God created Adam and Eve and came to live inside them, he gave them an original identity, which was like him. If you think about the idea of identity, it means who you are deep within yourself. It's not about things like your ethnicity, your personality type, or your looks. Identity means the deepest core of who and what you are. This is specifically who you are in your spirit, your human spirit. The part of you that is spiritual.

When we're told God created Adam and Eve in his image, it means he created them with the human identity that was full of his character. In that identity, they were perfectly righteous, patient, kind, loving, and holy, because they were the first partakers of God's divine nature since he was in them. That is what he intended for every human from the beginning, including you and me.

He told them in Genesis 2:16–17, "From any tree of the garden you may eat freely; but from the tree of the knowledge of good and evil you shall not eat, for in the day that you eat from it you will surely die" (NASB).

Then Satan showed up and twisted God's words to tempt Adam and Eve. The serpent said in Genesis 3:4–5, "You surely will not die! For God knows that in the day you eat from it your eyes will be opened, and you will be like God, knowing good and evil" (NASB).

Satan lied about more than one thing, but do you see the identity lie? He not only told Adam and Eve they would be like God; he told them they needed to do something to achieve that state. They needed to eat fruit from the forbidden tree. In essence, he was saying to them, "What God has done in giving you your original identity is incomplete. You are not enough. You need to do something to improve your identity. You can make yourself better through your performance even though it means disobeying God."

The moment Adam and Eve ate from the forbidden tree, Satan stole their identity in this sense: their perfect identity from God was exchanged for a flawed identity from Satan, an identity that was alive for one that was dead. As a result we are all born with this stolen identity. John 10:10 says, "The thief's purpose is to steal and kill and destroy" (NLT).

For those who don't have Christ in them, their identity remains dead, meaning in essence stolen. And they can't find it on their own. They need to place their faith in Jesus Christ to find it.

For those who know Christ, Satan continues to whisper the same lie he whispered to Adam and Eve about identity. He tells us what God has done for us is not enough. Because of our ignorance and confusion about our God-given identity, we can fall into the trap of believing him.

For instance, he told me God's salvation isn't sufficient. He whispered that I needed to do something more to improve on what God has done. I needed to become better. I needed to make myself complete. I needed to become enough. And the way to do that was to perform, which is also disobedience to God.

Today, when we buy in to this lie that we must improve on our God-given identity, Satan tricks us into believing spiritual identity theft has happened to us. We allow him to steal the truth of our identity in Christ and replace it with the lie of a false identity.

Has Satan tricked you with the same lie? Do you ever feel as though God's love and salvation aren't enough to make you into the kind of person you've always wanted to be? In all my years of counseling, I've found everyone feels this way on some level.

Living with an Identity Crisis

Joan came to see me for counseling as a Christian with a gnawing sense that she just wasn't good enough. Yet to meet her you would have thought the opposite. She had been the "good girl" growing up. She had won several beauty contests in her teens and twenties. She was a successful attorney. She had a loving husband and three children. To top it off, she was a leader for a national women's Bible study ministry.

By all outward appearances, she had a great life. But here she was sitting in front of me, wondering why all the things she had accomplished didn't satisfy her.

Joan had been a Christian since she was nine years old. Now she was thirty-nine. As Joan told her story, she described growing up with a mom who was always focused on the outer appearance. "You need to always look your best. You never know who might be watching you," was a common refrain. These comments were posed as if they would help Joan succeed in life, but they hurt rather than helped. Joan heard constant messages of disapproval, such as:

"Fix your hair for goodness' sake; it's a mess."

"Why did you put that blouse with that skirt?"

"Stop slouching. Stand up straight and confident."

When Joan met her mother's standard for outward appearance, something strange would happen. Her mother would shock her by saying, "You are so vain. All you do is look in the mirror." That was like a punch in Joan's emotional stomach. She just couldn't get it right with her mom either way.

Joan's dad was passive and uninvolved in her life. She longed for his attention and affirmation, but the main message she got was, "You're not important enough for me to spend time with you or talk with you." This message programmed her to believe there was something wrong with her. Specifically, she came to believe deep down that she was unlovable and ugly or her dad would have treated her differently.

The messages she tucked away about herself were "I am only as good as I look" and "I don't measure up" and "I can't do anything right." This not only reinforced her belief that she wasn't enough, but it added other wrinkles: "I am inadequate" and "I have to get it right or people will not like me."

Can you see how Joan's false identity was being formed? Yet one more important source influenced her view of herself as well— the church she grew up in. Joan's church believed and preached from the Bible, and she learned many things that were good. But intertwined with the good were messages that just were not true.

Almost every Sunday, Joan heard that she—and every other Christian—was just a "sinner saved by grace." In addition, her pastor frequently quoted Jeremiah 17:9: "The human heart is the most deceitful of all things, and desperately wicked. Who really knows how bad it is?" (NLT). Joan was told she could not trust her heart and that she was a desperately wicked person even though she was a Christian.

Because Joan believed these various messages, she determined to "fix" herself. She would work hard to try to make herself more lovable. She would excel to prove she was adequate. She would try to make God proud by being the best Christian she could be.

I wasn't surprised when Joan told me she often struggled with perfectionism. Perfectionism is fine if you are a brain surgeon; you need to be a perfectionist. But when it comes to relationships and everyday life, perfectionism can be toxic.

After Joan described her experiences to me, I said, "Everything you believe about yourself is the opposite of what God says about you. In other words, you're having an identity crisis. The identity you have been programmed to believe isn't from God. You have been living your life based on a false identity."

The Search for Your Stolen Identity

Can you relate to Joan's situation? If so, you are not alone. The good news is you have a true identity God wants you to discover. It will bring great healing and freedom in your life. In the next chapter, I want to start the process by helping you see your true identity from Scripture. My desire is that you agree with God about who you are, not with the other incorrect messages from unreliable sources as we are about to see.

Our human search for identity can lead us to mistakenly try to find it in other people and in ways that make the problem worse. Let's look at six key areas:

1. Parents

Tim was like every other child who looked to his parents to try to find out who he was. His problem was that his dad was an alcoholic.

When Tim's dad got drunk, he would say, "You will never amount to anything. You are a sorry excuse for a son. I wish I'd never even had you."

These comments from Tim's father formed a negative view of his identity. Years later, when Tim came to me for counseling, he had already destroyed two marriages, even though he was a Christian.

Like Tim, you and I begin our identity search hoping that our parents will tell us who we are. You may have grown up in a home like Tim's where you experienced a tremendous amount of rejection. Maybe it was so bad that you were told you'd never amount to anything, and you have spent your entire life so far either trying to prove your parents were wrong or you have simply given in to that false identity, accepting that they were right.

On the other hand, you may have grown up with wonderful parents who loved you, encouraged you, and told you how proud they were of you. In fact, you might go so far as to say you have a "good self-image." Be careful, though. If your parents did not raise you to know your identity in Christ, you haven't truly found your stolen identity.

2. Friends

Jackson grew up in a loving Christian home. School was a different story, though. On the playground kids called him all kinds of names, especially when he began to wear glasses and braces. He heard comments like, "Hey, freak! What's up, Metal Mouth? Have you bitten anybody lately? Don't come over here with us, Four Eyes. We don't want you around."

Those words were deeply wounding to Jackson, but the wounds went even deeper when his friends joined in. When they came over to his house to play, they acted totally different. He was confused, but the messages were clear. And his friends confirmed it: "You're not like everybody else. You're a reject."

Like Jackson, we can also look to our friends to help us find our stolen identity. We hope they will tell us who we are. We believe if we have their acceptance, that will prove we are wonderful people. We try to perform in sports, music, grades, or clubs, or just screw up with the misfits. We try to wear the right kinds of clothes. We try to impress with our phone, our car, our house, or a boat. Yet this is a fleeting identity based on the opinions of others, rather than on God's opinion. How much do you strive to gain the approval of your friends?

3. The Past

If you had good circumstances in your past, you may believe those former experiences define who you are to this day. This reminds me of a group of retired NFL players who were honored at their former team's game at halftime. One of the players was a friend of mine. He said player after retired player told him how they really missed the roar of the crowd. They had gained their identity from playing, which still defined them.

In contrast, if you don't like your past, you might do everything in your power to hide it and avoid thinking about it. I talked with a twenty-something young man named Carl who had his entire life ahead of him. He wanted to get a good job, get married, have kids, and serve in his church. But he confided in me that one thing was holding him back: his past. He had been sentenced to prison wrongly when he lived in Spain and stayed there for months before it all got straightened out. Although he had been out for years, he said, "I still see myself as an ex-con. I didn't commit the crime, but I feel guilty for hanging with the wrong crowd of troublemakers." He had tagged himself with that identity and it was holding him back.

Are you letting your past define you?

4. Social Media

"I hate Facebook!" Jane said in her first counseling session. "You have to present yourself as never having any problems."

Jane went on to tell me her life was anything but great. She was divorced and her kids were in their thirties but still lived with her. They gave her a lot of trouble, and money was always a problem.

On Facebook, though, Jane was another person. She pretended her life was great. She would always get a lot of "likes" and positive comments. The problem was none of her posts were true!

The rise of social media has given many people the opportunity to connect with old friends and new ones. It can be fun—unless you use it to try to find your stolen identity. Tallying how many "likes" you have on Facebook compared to your other friends is an insidious problem. Also, it's easy to look for affirmation or adulation in hopes of bolstering your sense of who you are. God forbid what might happen to your identity if you accidentally deleted your account!

Do you enhance your image on social media by posting only pictures, vacation details, or stories that make you look good? Are you envious of others when reading their posts?

5. Performance

I was reading an interview with the famous singer Michael Jackson. In it he was asked why he went on tours and performed for thousands of people at a time. I must give him credit, because his answer was brutally honest. He said what most of us think about our own performance in life, though we may never be on a stage like he was. He said he did it for people's acceptance.

After you finish school, you have to perform for your boss at work to keep your job or to get a promotion. Maybe you've learned to perform at church by serving faithfully. Or maybe you've performed just trying to obey God, hoping he would be impressed and others would too. Nothing is wrong with any of those pursuits, unless you are using them to try to find your stolen identity.

I'll be honest. I've been in full-time ministry for years, and before I knew who I really was, I remember more than once making sure I let it slip how much I prayed—secretly hoping to impress people. Yeah, I know that behavior sounds twisted, because praying is not for the purpose of finding your identity.

In what areas do you tend to perform the most to get other people's attention and approval?

6. Possessions

Jimmy came to me for counseling in hopes that he wouldn't go to jail. He had broken his probation by taking a trip out of state, and now his probation officer was asking him to turn himself in. He was scared. He wanted help finding out why he kept breaking the law.

I asked Jimmy to tell me a little about his growing up. He described how he was raised in government housing and his family never had much. He saw the drug dealers riding around in nice new cars and wanted to have nice things too. But he didn't want to get involved with drug dealers, so he decided to steal nice things from homes in wealthy neighborhoods.

During one of his earlier times in jail, Jimmy became a Christian. He knew stealing was a sin, but he just couldn't stop himself. I suspected his problem was an identity problem more than a stealing problem.

"Jimmy, why do you think you steal?" I asked him.

"Because I want things I can't afford to buy."

"I understand that, Jimmy. But I suspect this goes deeper than just wanting things you can't buy. You don't sell them, do you?"

"No, most of the time I don't."

"Tell me how you feel about yourself when you get these things you steal."

"Well, I feel good at first, believing that I am somebody now. I'm not just some poor sucker who grew up in government housing. I am somebody because I have stuff. But then, since I've become a Christian, that good feeling is replaced by deep grieving."

I now knew Jimmy stood on the precipice of realizing why he kept stealing. "Let me tell you what I think is going on here. In your mind, you have a view of yourself that I term your personal identity. It's who you think you are deep down. Your identity seems to be that you are a poor person. When you steal things and enjoy them, you are trying to recreate yourself to have a different identity—no longer a poor person but a special person."

Jimmy had a lightbulb moment and said, "I've never understood that before, but I see exactly what you are saying. I'm getting my identity from my lack of possessions or my ownership of possessions."

Just like Jimmy, whether you have a lot of money or a little money, you can easily let it define you.

All kinds of people come for counseling and to hear me teach. Some have been wealthy and some have been poor and many have been in between. In almost every case, though, they were still trying to find their stolen identity. That's one reason they were emotionally or relationally in trouble.

I'm reminded of an interview I saw with one of the richest women in America, Eileen Rockefeller. She said something amazing and shocking: "It doesn't matter if we have money or don't have money; we suffer in our own ways. And the net worth of our bank account is not nearly so important, ultimately, as the self-worth."[1]

1. "Growing Up Rockefeller," CBS News, September 16, 2013, http://www.cbs news.com/news/growing-up-rockefeller/2/.

How to Identify Your Identity Lie

I want to help you discover what is holding your false identity together. I call it "the lie" you believe about yourself. You may have picked this lie up as a child, teen, or adult, but it's the wheel upon which your false identity turns.

At a conference where I was teaching, I asked a small group to share a lie they believed about themselves. It was fascinating to hear the lies Satan had whispered—a different one to each individual. Here are just a few:

I'm better than everyone else.

I'm invisible.

I'm one big screwup.

I'm not masculine enough.

I'm a whore.

I'm a success.

I'm inadequate.

I'm a mistake.

I'm the life of the party.

Do you know what lie Satan whispers to you?

If the truth sets us free, then lies keep us in bondage. That's why it's essential that you identify what lies could be affecting you. We all believe more than one lie, yet over and over I've seen people with one core lie from which the others fan out like spokes on a bicycle wheel.

Here are a few steps you can take to help you discover your core lie. Keep in mind that this lie is the complete opposite of what your heavenly Father thinks about you. It's the same hook Satan used with Adam and Eve when they ate from the tree in the garden of Eden. Here's an important clue:

Your core lie will always involve some kind of performance to make yourself acceptable to yourself, others, or even God.

This lie gets inserted into your mind directly from Satan or through the voice of a person in your life. It may have initially happened during a particular event in your past. This lie is then whispered by Satan to you over and over at various times.

From my experience, I've found the quickest way to identify your core lie is to ask God to show you what it is directly. Why don't you give it a try? Ask God this question: *Father, would you please show me what my core lie is about my identity?*

Sit in silence and wait. Consider the thoughts that come to mind, even if you are not 100 percent clear about what they mean. Write them down somewhere.

When I asked God this question several years ago, he impressed upon me that my core lie was "I must be the best to be important."

You can see how my lie put me at the center of my own life as my own source of defining my personal identity. That is a tiring way to live, believe me. I walked in that lie for years. It generated a lot of pressure that brought a lot of anxiety. I felt good temporarily when I performed up to the standards that I set, but I also felt bad the numerous times I failed.

Once you know your core lie, how does it make you feel? Tired, anxious, depressed, superior, relieved, prideful, and so on? Ask God to reveal what kinds of activities and behaviors you've done because of that lie.

Now that you see your core lie and understand how it makes you feel and realize how it has caused you to perform, you can probably understand why you have felt so frustrated and exhausted at times.

But take heart! Your heavenly Father knows the truth about you, and it has nothing to do with your performance. Best of all, God's view of you is astonishingly better than anything you could ever imagine!

To Whom Do You Listen?

Tony was a baseball player who had been a fantastic college hitter. He had a great average and hit many home runs. All through his life, his dad had helped Tony learn how to play this favorite American pastime. He not only taught Tony, but he also told him he was a great player and would go far if he wanted.

A major league professional team drafted him and put him in their Triple-A league, which is where most players learn how to play on that club's "preparation" team. Tony immediately made an impact, leading the league in hits and home runs. Upper management was so impressed by his abilities that they quickly sent him up to their major league team.

A strange thing happened, though. Tony suddenly couldn't hit like he did before. His performance was mediocre, at best. The coach chalked it up to rookie jitters, believing he would do better his second year. But he didn't. This went on for a few seasons, until one day he couldn't take it any longer.

Tony called his dad and said, "I'm quitting. I just can't stand not being able to hit the ball like I used to." After a few moments of silence, his dad said, "Don't you quit! Let them kick you off the team, but don't you quit." His dad then reminded Tony of his lifelong opinion of him as a great baseball player.

Tony hung up and started believing who his dad said he was and acted on it. He watched videos of his swing. He practiced at home. And in a few weeks he began to return to the high level of hitting that had been normal for him. His coach asked him what made the difference. Tony replied that it was all because his dad told him not to quit and believed in him.

Later Tony shared his story in a prison setting, telling the inmates how important his dad had been in his life. He encouraged the men to still be in their kids' lives despite their incarceration. Afterward, one prisoner stayed behind to talk to him. Here's what he said:

"That's great that your dad told you who you were and how you lived up to what he said about you. My father did that, too, but in a different way. He told me my whole life that I was no good and I would never amount to anything. I lived up to who he said I would be. That's why I'm here today, in prison."

Friend, which voice have you been listening to about your identity? Have you been listening to Satan or your Father, God himself?

Satan wants to destroy you with lies about who you are. He stole your original identity. He doesn't want you to know the truth so you will spend your entire life desperately trying to find out who you are.

Your heavenly Father, however, isn't going to let Satan keep the truth of your wonderful identity hidden from you. God wants to bring it out into the open. He wants you to enjoy all he created you to be. He has a fantastic opinion of you. But if you don't know it, you'll be listening to Satan as he whispers all kinds of destructive lies and opinions about you.

When you begin to understand how Jesus restored your stolen identity in the New Covenant, it may sound almost too good to be true. But it is true. That's the aspect of his best-kept secret you'll discover in the next chapter.

4

Christians Don't Have a Civil War Raging inside Them

Drew sat down in front of me as a beaten-down, middle-aged man. I could tell by the circles under his eyes and the unhappiness on his face that he was miserable. When I asked him to share why he came for counseling, he said, "I'm having marital problems, and I want help." He talked about how he and his wife, Kono, fought with each other and argued a lot about money and their finances. He said their three kids were starting to act up because of their arguing.

As we discussed his marital problems in more depth, however, Drew revealed the real reason he and his wife fought so much: he had a cocaine addiction. Before he became a Christian, Drew had used cocaine habitually. But after becoming a Christian, he had not used cocaine until recently.

Drew said, "Kono and I had a good marriage. But then I started feeling a lot of stress from my job, and I made some bad financial choices, which put us in a great amount of debt. I was tempted to do cocaine again to deal with the stress. I prayed, read my Bible, and even fasted to try avoiding the temptation. But those things worked for only a couple of weeks. Finally, one day I skipped work, got the cocaine, and used it at home while Kono was at her job.

"Afterward, I promised God and myself I wouldn't do it again. But a week later, I slipped up again and got some more cocaine. Kono came home early and caught me. She went ballistic, and we started arguing. After things calmed down, I promised her I'd never do it again.

"But three weeks ago, I went on a one-week binge. I called in sick to work, disappeared, and spent ten thousand dollars on cocaine. When I returned home, Kono threatened to kick me out of the house. So that is why I'm here today, because I know she's right. Even though I'm a Christian and I truly love Jesus, I need help."

"Drew, I appreciate your honesty," I said. "I cannot personally help you, but Jesus definitely can. With that in mind, my next few questions are crucial. First, do you believe you are addicted to cocaine?"

"Yes," he said.

"Do you believe your addiction is a sin?"

"Yes, I sure do."

"Is it possible that you have learned to cope with stress and negative feelings by your addiction to cocaine?"

"Yes, I can see that perspective now that we've discussed it."

I pressed further. "When you feel the temptation to do cocaine, do you feel as though two sides within you are battling each other? For instance, do you tell yourself you don't want to do cocaine, but also feel attracted to the temptation? In other words, do you feel as though a civil war is going on inside of you?"

"Yes, exactly!" Drew exclaimed. "And it scares me to feel so hypocritical inside. I thought being a Christian was supposed to help get rid of temptation. Instead I almost feel like there is a good

Drew who is getting overmatched by a bad Drew. I want to do the right thing, but I still seem to do the wrong thing. I feel like I'm fighting against myself, and it's so depressing."

Drew's situation is similar to what many Christians feel about life today—stuck and hopeless. A major part of this problem is that they don't know who they really are.

This is an alarming problem, because true identity is one of the most central truths God wants us to know. The Bible shouts this truth so loudly that you can't miss it. But a confusing misconception can lead many Christians, just like Drew, to doubt their true identity. The misconception is the cunning lie from Satan that we are holy and evil at the same time.

Is a Civil War Raging inside You?

Do you ever feel as though two equal powers are inside you with completely opposite desires? This is a common feeling, which seems to explain how we struggle to live a life that pleases God.

For example, when a lustful thought enters your mind, you know you shouldn't give in to temptation. But as a Christian, there's also a desire within you to say no to the temptation. In Ezekiel 36:26, God says he has given us a new heart that desires righteous living.

> I will give you a new heart—I will give you new and right desires—and put a new spirit within you. I will take out your stony hearts of sin and give you new hearts of love. (TLB)

If that's the case, though, then why does a sinister, opposite desire to give in to temptation seem to be within us—even when we know we'll regret it? What or who is this other player inside of us?

I remember hearing as a young Christian that I had two natures, the "old self" and the "new self," living inside of me.

The "old self" is the spiritual identity we were born with because of Adam's original sin. It's the deepest core of who we are when we show up on planet Earth. It's the identity we inherited from Adam when he died spiritually in the garden of Eden. It's what gives us the identity of being sinners and even enemies of God. It's the essence of who we are in Adam. The reality is that every person born after Adam is a spiritual zombie—alive on the outside but dead on the inside.

Ephesians 2:1–2 says it this way: "You were dead in your trespasses and sins, in which you formerly walked according to the course of this world, according to the prince of the power of the air, of the spirit that is now working in the sons of disobedience" (NASB).

As we will see, the Bible says our "old self" is no longer in play after we become Christians.

You may also hear people talk about the "new self." The "new self" is the new spiritual identity we get from Jesus Christ. It is now the new deepest core of who and what we are. It is the identity we received through being born again. We are no longer dead in Adam but alive in our identity in Christ.

We see this later in Ephesians 2:4–5: "Because of his great love for us, God, who is rich in mercy, made us alive with Christ even when we were dead in transgressions—it is by grace you have been saved."

Jesus described this transformation when he spoke to a Jewish religious leader named Nicodemus. He told Nicodemus he had been born with the wrong identity even though he was a spiritual leader to the Jewish people in his day. John 3:3 says, "Jesus replied, 'Very truly I tell you, no one can see the kingdom of God unless they are born again.'"

This new birth Jesus spoke of happens the moment a person believes in him for their salvation. The new birth is the spiritual birth of the new self. It is our new identity in Christ.

But . . . I once thought these two "selves" existed side by side, like two opposite "Marks" inside of me—a good Mark and a bad Mark. It sort of sounded right, but it was also very confusing. Many Christians have the same misconception. Let's clear up the confusion once and for all.

The Two-Dog Debate

Some people may tell you your old self is like a ferocious dog living inside of you, terrorizing you and other people. It controls you and makes you commit all kinds of sins. It's what makes you selfish, self-centered, and dependent on yourself instead of God. It's the reason you are tempted and the reason you sin.

In contrast, they say the new self is like a wonderful, loving dog that always wants to be with you. It protects you and leads you to do what God wants. It's why you want to live a righteous life. It's why you want to serve and help others. It's the reason you can resist temptation and obey God.

According to this illustration, the dog (or "self") you feed the most will be the one that wins the battle in your daily life. To feed the old self usually means things like watching pornography, hanging out with people who cuss, getting drunk, going to clubs, having sex outside of marriage, or just avoiding God. Feeding the new self means doing things like reading the Bible, praying, listening to good sermons, serving God, and donating money.

This two-self teaching seems to express what we often experience, doesn't it? Some will use Scriptures that seem to prove this, like Ephesians 4:22–24, which says,

> In reference to your former manner of life, you lay aside the old self, which is being corrupted in accordance with the lusts of deceit, and that you be renewed in the spirit of your mind, and put on the new self, which in the likeness of God has been created in righteousness and holiness of the truth. (NASB)

If you look closely at the text, though, you'll notice these verses are clearly speaking about behavior. When it says, "your former manner of life, you lay aside the old self," it means to get rid of the sinful behaviors that were a part of the old self that is no longer inside of you. Then putting on the new self is about living with righteous behavior that is consistent with the new self you now have, meaning the new identity in Christ you have today.

Jesus Has Replaced Your Identity

Two-self teaching has two big problems.

First, it's not helpful. I've asked many people whether this teaching has helped them overcome a specific sin, provided emotional healing, or repaired a ruptured relationship. Not one person has ever been able to show how the two-self concept produced those fruits. Why? Because it's not God's truth!

Which leads to the second problem: it's not biblical. The Bible tells us we have only one self. For example, Romans 6:6 says, "We know that our old self was crucified with him so that the body ruled by sin might be done away with, that we should no longer be slaves to sin."

The Greek language gives us an understanding much clearer than English does. The verb *crucified* is a specific aorist tense. It means the old self, or what some call the old nature, was in Christ when he died on the cross. In other words, your old self died with him on the cross. Notice that it's past tense, meaning it has already happened. And the Greek tense tells us it happened once and for all. It is done. It will never be repeated.

Not only that, but Romans 6:4–5 tells us when we were buried with Christ, our old self was buried with Christ. When Jesus rose from the grave, he left our old self in that grave.

We were therefore buried with him through baptism into death in order that, just as Christ was raised from the dead through the

64

glory of the Father, we too may live a new life. For if we have been united with him in a death like his, we will certainly also be united with him in a resurrection like his.

Jesus will never die on a cross again, so your old self will never die on a cross in him again. It's a done deal. The old self is not going to rise up out of the tomb where it was buried with Jesus. It's been left there forever. Let me be clear. Once we are saved, we definitely do *not* have the old self—or old nature for those who use that term—living in us. That old "you" is gone forever! He or she is not ever going to rise from the grave like so many are often told. When you became a Christ follower, something amazing happened that goes all the way back to when Jesus died on the cross. You also died with Christ. In other words, your old self died along with Jesus on the cross.

When Jesus was raised from the dead, God created a brand-new self, a new you that was resurrected with him. He replaced your old identity from Adam with your new identity in Christ.

This resurrected new self is clarified in a familiar verse, 2 Corinthians 5:17: "Therefore, if anyone is in Christ, the new creation has come: the old has gone, the new is here!"

The phrase *new creation* means a new species, which says there are two kinds of humans in the world today. Spiritually speaking, some have their identity still in Adam and some have their identity now in Christ. Let me circle back to Galatians 2:20, to make this clearer. Paul said, "I have been crucified with Christ and I no longer live, but Christ lives in me. The life I now live in the body, I live by faith in the Son of God, who loved me and gave himself for me."

For many years, when I read that verse, I thought it was speaking of a spiritual state I would arrive at one day, putting me on the highest plane of the Christian life. If you step back and read the verse carefully, however, you see it's talking about something God has *already* done to us that affects our present life. Let me personalize Galatians 2:20 for you by inserting a few words to give it real meaning:

> I [insert your name], [the old me in Adam], have been crucified [past tense] with Christ and I [the old me in Adam] no longer live, but Christ lives in me [the new me in Christ]. The life I [the new me in Christ] now live in the body, I live by faith in the Son of God [who is in me], who loved me and gave himself for me.

Do you see the difference? Do you see what God has already finished? The old self is gone and there is only one self—the new you in Christ!

The Old Self and the Flesh Are Not the Same

Another way Christians get confused is by incorrectly assuming the "old self" and a term called "the flesh" are the same. I will discuss the flesh in chapter 10, but let me define it briefly for now and distinguish between the two terms.

First, the word *flesh* in Scripture does not mean the human body in the majority of verses. Instead, the flesh is a spiritual term that means all the ways people use their bodies and personalities in sinful ways as a result of not depending on God. The word *flesh* represents all the ways people have learned to cope with life's challenges apart from dependence on Christ. The flesh also means living as if we are separated from God, though as Christians we are united with him. In other words, living as if we aren't Christians although we are Christians.

When people don't have Christ in them, they live according to the flesh all the time. The reason is because the old self is 100 percent sinful and motivates them to develop patterns of the flesh.

As we've seen, Christians do not have the old self as their core identity. They have only the new self. Christians do have the flesh, but it can't be the old self. As Christians, however, we can still live independently without relying on God. When we do, we live according to the "flesh."

As a result of this confusion, we can misunderstand Scripture like Romans 7:17–18, thinking it is referring to the old self fighting against the new self, when it says, "So now, no longer am I the one doing it, but sin which dwells in me. For I know that nothing good dwells in me, that is, in my flesh; for the willing is present in me, but the doing of the good is not" (NASB).

If you believe the "old self" and the "flesh" are the same, you will immediately think these verses mean the old self is fighting against the new self. But that's impossible since the old self is long gone. We still deal with the flesh, but it's not the old self in us.

Your Birth, Not Your Behavior, Determines Your Identity

Consider the difference between the two following statements:

Culture tells you your behavior defines your identity.

God tells you your birth defines your identity.

Unfortunately, we teach people—even children—that behavior determines their identity. For example, if your son picks up his toys, you might say, "You're a good boy." If your daughter hugs her sister, you might say, "You're a good girl."

The reality, however, is that little children are born sinners. Have you ever noticed you don't have to teach your kids to be selfish? They grab their toy from another child and say emphatically, "Mine!" You don't have to teach them how to lie, either. As soon as you confront those cute little faces with what they did wrong, they don't say, "Oh, Mom, of course I hit my brother. You are so wise and wonderful. I will always tell you the truth." Instead children begin to conjure up excuses right in front of you.

You and I were born sinners. John 8:44 describes how Jesus even told the most religious people of his day, the Pharisees, that their father was the devil. And this is true of everyone, whether you are religious or rebellious.

The moment you placed your faith in Jesus as your Savior, however, you experienced a second birth. This new birth made you a child of God. John 1:12 says, "To all who believed him and accepted him, he gave the right to become children of God" (NLT).

Have you ever read about the early church in 1 Corinthians? Their behavior wasn't just bad; it was horrible! They claimed superiority based on whether Apollos or Paul led them to Christ, which produced jealousy. Imagine meeting for worship back then. Everyone who was led to Christ by Apollos sat on the left side, while everyone led to Christ by Paul sat on the right side. Sounds crazy, doesn't it?

The Bible even describes a man and his stepmother in this particular church living together and having sex with each other. But no one would confront them. The congregation pretended everything was okay. They may have even said, "They're under grace, so their sinful behavior doesn't matter."

When this Corinthian church met to celebrate communion, which you may know as the Eucharist or the Lord's Supper, each person brought food and wine for a big picnic. The group was not only ethnically and socially diverse, it was financially diverse. The rich people brought a lot of food, but they selfishly hoarded it and refused to share with the poorer members. Some of them even drank so much wine during the celebration that they got drunk.

Listen to me closely. If there was ever a place where God could use behavior to define a Christian, this Corinthian church would be it. Yet do you know what Paul calls these Christians? He didn't call them sinners, backsliders, losers, or heathens. In 1 Corinthians 1:2, he shockingly called them saints:

To the church of God which is at Corinth, to those who have been sanctified in Christ Jesus, saints by calling, with all who in every place call on the name of our Lord Jesus Christ, their Lord and ours. (NASB)

We tend to think of a "saint" as someone who lives a particularly godly life, such as a grandmother who prays for her family her entire life. Depending on your background, you may think of a saint as someone who does all that plus a miracle or two, and after they die a group of people gets together and bestows upon them the title "saint."

But the word *saint* simply means a holy person. This is what God calls the Corinthians, but it's not based on their behavior. It's based on their new birth in Christ.

God calls you a saint too. Are you willing to believe it? He calls you a saint based on your new birth in Christ, not because of your behavior. In fact, God calls you a saint over sixty times in the New Testament.

Why don't you stop right now and say out loud to God and to yourself, "God, because you say I am a saint, I agree with you. I *am* a saint!"

Now, you might be thinking, *Mark, that sounds kind of weird. If you only knew what I did last Saturday night, you would know I'm not a saint. And I definitely don't feel like a saint.* My opinion of you, though, would remain the same based on God's perspective: "Yes, you are a saint if you are in Christ, regardless of what you did or whether you feel like one."

You Are Not a Sinner and a Saint

You may recall that at the beginning of the previous chapter, I asked whether a Christian can be a liar, a thief, an alcoholic, a drug addict, a homosexual, or a sinner. I hope you see now that though Christians can lie, steal, get drunk, do drugs, have sex with someone of the same gender, and commit all kinds of sins, those behaviors don't define them. The reality is that if they do those things, they are saints who are lying, stealing, getting drunk, doing drugs, having same-gender sex, and sinning.

You may be wondering about 1 Timothy 1:15, where Paul states, "This is a trustworthy saying, and everyone should accept it: 'Christ Jesus came into the world to save sinners'—and I am the worst of them all" (NLT).

Isn't Paul saying that even though he is a Christian, he is still a sinner? No, he's not saying that at all. The verses before and after tell us he was speaking of his life *before* he became a Christian.

This doesn't mean Christians don't sin. It just means sinning doesn't define them as sinners. In other words, though you were saved by grace, you are not a sinner saved by grace. You are also not a sinner and a saint. You are just a saint.

When my children were young, I heard a big commotion with yelling and running. My son Ben was chasing his younger brother, Christopher, and yelling, "You're a tattletale! You're a tattletale! I'm going to get you!" Ben had been disciplined by my wife because Christopher told her something Ben did, and he wasn't happy about it.

Somehow Christopher's little legs were going so fast that Ben's long arms couldn't catch him. But Ben kept yelling those same words at him until Christopher finally yelled back over his shoulder, "I'm not a tattletale! I'm a truth teller!" To have the last word, Ben said, "Well, you're a truth teller who tattletales!"

That's like what God says about us. We are saints who commit different kinds of sins, but we are still saints!

Your Ethnicity Is Not Your Identity

Ethnicity is important when it comes to understanding our identity. Christians can celebrate their ethnicity because God gave it to each of us. We must realize, however, that ethnicity is not what ultimately defines us as Christians. Our identity in Christ is what defines us in the deepest way. Are you someone with black-, white-, brown-, yellow-, or red-pigmented skin who is also a Christian? No, it's the reverse. You are a child of God who has your particular skin color and ethnicity.

Sexual Attractions, Sexual Sins, and Gender Identity Feelings Don't Define Your Identity

My staff and I have counseled many Christians struggling with attraction to the same gender, internet pornography, sexual lust for the opposite gender, and sexual fantasies, along with other sexual sins. We listen with compassion to each of these Christians as they share their struggles with us.

One of the great things we share with them is that our sexual sins, sexual lusts, and sexual attractions do not define who we are. Our identity in Christ defines who we are instead.

Fred shared with me in his first counseling session that he felt attracted to other men, though he had never acted on it. He concluded from this that he was a homosexual. I still remember the relief on his face when I told him that he wasn't a homosexual but was who God said he is in Christ.

I read to him 1 Corinthians 6:9–11 (which is in the beginning of chapter 3 in this book). I explained to him that though he was once a homosexual before he was a Christian, now he was a forgiven, righteous, holy child of God. He immediately felt hopeful and went on to experience great freedom from this struggle as he continued the counseling.

The same is true for others. You are not defined by your identity as a lustful person, an adulterous person, an immoral person, a transgender person, a gay person, a lesbian, a bisexual, etc. If you have received God's salvation through Jesus Christ, your sexual attraction and sin don't define you. You are who God says you are—a righteous, holy child of God, just as I shared with Fred.

A related truth is that you are not defined by how you feel about your gender identity, though one social media company now asks people to choose from seventy-one gender options. This is simply another attempt to find the identity that was taken from us in the garden. If you are a Christ follower, you are defined by your identity in Christ.

You Are Already a Godly Person in Christ

I'm so grateful that God showed me the truth about him and my identity. Since then, I've experienced more peace in my life, and I don't have to let my behavior and mistakes define my identity. Yet I still had this nagging voice in my head that occasionally whispered, "I need to become a godly man." It was like a buzzing mosquito that wouldn't leave me alone.

One day I was alone in my car, driving to work and thinking about what it meant to be a godly man—just as I had for many years. In that moment, though, God whispered something in my spirit. He said, "Mark, you are already a godly man. Do you believe me?"

As I accepted that truth for the first time, it seemed as if everything around me suddenly got brighter and a heavy weight fell away from my shoulders. I realized God was saying, "You have been a godly man since the day you were saved at age nine." Now I could stop doing spiritual activities to prove I was a godly man, because I already was godly based on my identity in Christ. To be quite honest, that moment provided one of the greatest feelings of relief I've ever experienced. For the first time I felt as though I could relax before God. My striving to be a godly man was over.

As I've counseled, taught, and preached in churches, I've discovered many Christians are stuck in the same place. They don't realize they are already godly, holy, righteous, loving, and patient in Christ. So they strive to become that person when they already are that person. Talk about living with a false identity.

Friend, more than anything, I want you to experience the same freedom God offers all of us. Are you ready to let go of a false identity based on your behavior, feelings, and the opinions of others? Are you ready to embrace your true identity in Christ?

Your True Identity in Christ

God's opinion of you is amazing! He wants you to live with a biblical self-image rather than a poor self-image or a narcissistic self-image. A biblical self-image is a great self-image! Here are just a few examples of God's opinions about you.

——My Identity in Christ——

Because I am in Christ . . .

I Am Lovable

I am a child of God—John 1:12
I am beloved—Romans 9:25
I am chosen—Colossians 3:12
I am loved by God as much as Jesus is—John 17:23, 26
I am Jesus's friend—John 15:15
I am inseparable from God's love—Romans 8:37–39

I Am Acceptable

I am accepted by God—Romans 15:7
I am righteous—2 Corinthians 5:21
I am a saint—1 Corinthians 1:2; Ephesians 1:1 (NASB)
I am not condemned—Romans 8:1
I am completely forgiven—Colossians 2:13
I am holy and blameless—Ephesians 1:4

I Am Valuable

I am God's masterpiece—Ephesians 2:10 (NLT)
I am adopted—Ephesians 1:5
I am God's treasure—Matthew 13:44
I am God's pearl—Matthew 13:45–46
I am a new creation—2 Corinthians 5:17
I am designed by God—Psalm 139:13–16

I Am Secure

I am more than a conqueror—Romans 8:37
I am complete in Christ—Colossians 2:10
I am safe in Christ—Colossians 3:3–4
I am seated in the heavenly realms—Ephesians 2:6
I am eternally in Christ—John 10:28
I am united with Christ—1 Corinthians 6:17

But what about Bible verses that make us sound as though we're evil and sinful? For example, some Christians get stuck on Jeremiah 17:9, which Joan brought up in chapter 3: "The human heart is the most deceitful of all things, and desperately wicked. Who really knows how bad it is?" (NLT).

How do we reconcile this verse with all the others I just listed? Here's the answer: Jeremiah 17:9 and the description of an evil heart was true before you received Christ as your Savior. But once you did, God removed that wicked heart and gave you a new one, which is good as we saw in Ezekiel 36:26. Isn't that a big relief?

Defeat Lies about Who You Are with the Truth

Remember the story of Drew at the beginning of this chapter? He was addicted to cocaine and believed he had two natures fighting inside of him. In other words, he didn't know who he really was according to God's perspective.

As I counseled Drew, I asked him, "Have you taken on the identity that you're an addict because of your addiction?"

"Yes, of course, especially based on some of the recovery programs I've attended," he said. "I still believe I'm a recovering cocaine addict."

I took a different approach and said, "Drew, I understand why recovery programs have people say, 'Hi, my name is Drew. I am an addict.' They want people who believe they can stop their addiction anytime to come out of their denial. But as Christians, we need to approach it differently. We need to say, 'Hi, my name is Drew. I am a child of God who is sinning through my addiction.' Here is the important difference. God does not define us as Christians by our behavior. God defines us by our birth."

I then explained to him what I've told you in this chapter. To make sure Drew saw the difference, I continued, "Do you see who God says you really are? Do you understand how this truth can free you from your addiction?"

"Yes, I sure do. If my identity is that of an addict, the most normal thing for me to do would be to live addicted. But if my identity is that of a child of God who is a saint, the most normal thing for me to do would be to live free from my addiction."

Ingrained habits and chemical dependencies, however, don't disappear overnight. So I continued counseling sessions with Drew to reinforce God's truth into his daily decision-making process.

One day Drew came in to see me. He was extremely excited. He said, "Mark, I get it! I finally get it! I see what you have been trying to tell me all this time. I am the righteousness of God in Christ, not a sinner. I am not what I do. I am who God says I am. I am a child of God, not an addict. I am a saint, not an addict. I am more than a conqueror in Christ, not an addict!"

"You've got it, Drew!" I said. "Now when you are tempted to do cocaine, you can fight that temptation with God's truth."

Drew and I met several more times to make certain he was successfully defeating his temptations to do cocaine. At each session, he would excitedly tell me how he had defeated those temptations by praying a prayer similar to this:

Lord, I am being tempted to do cocaine because I feel stressed right now. But I know I am not an addict. According to your Word, I am a child of God. I am complete in Christ. I am a conqueror in Christ. Jesus, I trust that because of who I am in you and who you are in me, I have victory over this temptation. Take care of this issue for me, Jesus.

About a year after Drew finished his counseling, he called me to say he had not done cocaine since we'd last met. He had been tempted several times, but he had relied on Jesus to defeat his temptation each time with the truth of his new identity in Christ.

As I did with Drew, allow me to ask you some challenging questions about your personal identity:

- Are you ready to let go of your false identity based on your past, your family, your failures, your successes, your friends, your marital status, your behavior, your sins, and so on?
- Do you agree that there is only one self or one core identity inside of you?
- Are you ready to agree with who God says you are?

If you struggle to see the difference between Satan's lies and God's view of you, here's a helpful exercise. On paper or in a digital document, write the word *Lies* in one column. Under that word write a list of the lies you believe about who you are.

Next, write the word *Truth* in a column next to the first one. In that column, write statements and Scripture references about who you are in Christ. Counteract as many lies as you can identify with truth and add to that list as you become aware of more lies.

Here are some personal lies you might believe as opposed to the truth God wants you to believe. Hopefully this will help get you started.

Lies	Truth	
I am a racist.	I am a grace-ist in Christ.	Galatians 3:28
I am a sexist.	I am an equality advocate in Christ.	Galatians 3:28
I am a classist.	I am unbiased in Christ.	Galatians 3:28
I am a greedy person.	I am a giver in Christ.	2 Corinthians 9:7
I am impatient.	I am patient in Christ.	Galatians 5:22
I am a screwup.	I am perfect in Christ.	Hebrews 10:14
I am a liar.	I am a truth teller in Christ.	Ephesians 4:25
I am a bitter person.	I am a forgiver in Christ.	Ephesians 4:32
I am unloving.	I am loving in Christ.	Galatians 5:22

If you struggle to identify the lies, examine your feelings. Feelings always follow thoughts. When you have a negative feeling, pray and say, "Jesus, please help me understand why I feel this way and what belief is behind the feeling." Then wait and write down what he reveals to you.

For example, if you feel depressed one day, ask Jesus to help identify why. He may show you you've been comparing yourself to someone else. That comparison is causing you to believe you are inferior, which is causing you to *feel* inferior. Jesus may even remind you that comparing yourself to others started in your childhood or at another point in your life. In this case, you could write under the *Lies* column, "I am inferior." Then under the *Truth* column, you could write, "I am complete in Christ—Colossians 2:10."

Continue these steps for every lie the Lord shows you going forward. Keep this list accessible, such as on your phone or computer, or tuck it in your Bible to review. Then when you experience negative feelings, go to Jesus and talk to him about it. Let him remind you what is true about who you are.

I encourage you to take this exercise a step further. Tape your list on your bathroom or closet mirror. Put a copy in your desk at work or in your car. As you see your list of lies and truths, pray through it silently or out loud. For example, pray daily, "Dear Father, I thank you that I am not a liar but a truth teller because of what Ephesians 4:25 says." You can do the same for the other lies mentioned above and any others God shows you. Use this exercise to start replacing all the lies you've held in your mind.

God wants you to enjoy the true identity he gave you when you became a Christian. As you allow God to reveal what already belongs to you, here is a suggested prayer:

> Father, because I didn't know my identity in Christ, I've spent all my life searching for my identity. As a result I've developed a false identity, which has controlled my life. Today I give up my false identity and choose to embrace by faith my true identity in Christ, regardless of the messages of my past, how I feel, or how I've been behaving. I choose to stop agreeing with Satan about who I am, and instead I choose to agree with who you say I am in Christ. Please give me understanding more and more about my true identity in Christ through the Holy Spirit who lives in me. Thank you for loving me so much as your child. In Jesus's name, Amen.

One of the best aspects of New Covenant Christianity is the reality that we have only one self, which is holy, loving, good, and complete in Christ. You no longer have to walk in Satan's lies or believe a false identity about yourself. Your identity has been fully restored. Walk in this truth today and experience the incredible freedom God offers!

5

Christians Are Just as Righteous as Jesus

Diego was a young man who walked into my counseling office looking despondent. He quietly said, "I've lost all joy for living. I used to look forward to getting up. Now every day is drudgery. I have no motivation. I barely make it through work, and my boss is getting angry with my lack of performance. I avoid my friends even though they keep calling me. I don't exercise and I'm gaining weight. And I've asked to be taken off the ministry team at my church that takes meals to families in need. But I still don't know why I've lost all joy for living I once had."

"Let's put your situation on a scale from 0 to 10," I replied. "If 0 is no depression and 10 is being so depressed you can't get out of bed, where are you most days on that scale?"

Diego thought for a minute and then said, "I'd say I'm about an 8."

"Tell me how you feel about your relationship with God," I said.

"I used to think it was really good. But, looking back, I realize that no matter how much I tried to obey God and serve him, I never

79

felt I measured up. In fact, I think when I die and go to heaven one day, Jesus will be hugging Billy Graham because he is so glad to see him. But when he sees me, I'm sure he'll stop smiling and tell me what a disappointment I am to him."

Diego's statements identify a common problem regarding God's acceptance that causes many Christians to struggle.

"Do you believe God loves you, Diego?"

"Yes," he said, "because that is what I have always been taught."

I approached it from a different direction and asked, "Do you believe God accepts you?"

"Well, it depends on the day. If I'm having a good day and obeying God, then I believe he accepts me. But on the days I sin, I don't believe he accepts me as much."

Diego is like many Christians I meet. He had a mental checklist and was working hard running on the treadmill of performing for God's acceptance, as well as the acceptance of his friends and his church. The problem with a treadmill, however, is that no matter how hard you work, you end up going nowhere. In other words, you never feel as though you have done enough to earn acceptance. Then the next day you have to get on the treadmill of performing for acceptance all over again.

How Righteous Do You Feel Right Now?

Because so many misunderstandings about the idea of righteousness occur, the concept has little meaning for many Christians. This truth, though, is the key to living every day with the confidence that our deepest God-given need for acceptance is fully met. More importantly, the truth of God's unconditional acceptance for you and me is tied directly to our righteousness.

Consider these pointed questions: How righteous do you feel as you read this book right now? Are you as righteous as the Christian you admire the most? Are you as righteous as your pastor? How about this question: Are you as righteous as Jesus Christ? Only those who are as righteous as Jesus Christ get into heaven. And only those as righteous as Jesus Christ can experience the peace of unconditional acceptance in this life. Yet if you have lived with a checklist mentality, as we discussed before, you may equate your righteousness with how well you fulfill your checklist each day.

We hear a lot in church about being righteous or having righteousness. Let's take a closer look at this truly amazing word.

Righteousness simply means to "be right." To be right in a spiritual sense means to be perfect. To be righteous, then, means to be perfect in God's opinion. The basis of his opinion regarding our righteousness is not only the criteria for heaven; it is the criteria for being able to enjoy the deepest intimacy possible with God and to live free in Christ now!

In the book of Romans, the idea of righteousness appears fifty times. Anytime God writes the same idea fifty times through one of the biblical writers we can be certain he's trying to get our attention.

I believe the reason is that God wants every Christian to know that the gift of righteousness brings the incredible blessings of full forgiveness of all our sins, freedom from our slavery to sin and Satan, and especially unconditional acceptance with God.

When You Are Justified, You Are Unconditionally Accepted

> Having been justified by faith, we have peace with God through our Lord Jesus Christ. (Rom. 5:1 NASB)

The word *justified* is from the same root word for righteousness. The core idea is that anyone who is justified is righteous.

Notice that the word *justified* is past tense, meaning it has already occurred. You will also notice it has happened to you and me. It is only true for those who believe in Jesus Christ. So because of Jesus

Christ and his life, death, burial, and resurrection, justification has been given to every person who believes in him.

To be justified means to be totally forgiven and to be made totally righteous. We who have faith in Jesus Christ have already been forgiven and made righteous. It's past tense. It's already happened to us.

Justified is also an accounting term telling us what our "righteousness account" is before God. Before salvation, we were not at zero; we were minus 100 percent! Do you know why? All the sins we have committed and will commit, along with our identity of being a sinner, put us 100 percent in the negative.

Can a person ever get above negative 100 percent through performance? This might include, for instance, trying to be a good person, obeying the Ten Commandments, attending church, giving away millions of dollars to feed the poor, or working at a soup kitchen. No! Regardless of what people do, they are eternally stuck at negative 100 percent. "No one is righteous—not even one" (Rom. 3:10 NLT).

When we place our faith in Christ for our salvation, all our sins are forgiven forever. In addition, our identity as a sinner is removed forever. This gets us to zero in our righteousness account with God. Yet what I've observed in all my years of talking with Christians is they believe the gospel gets them only to zero. Think of it this way. If you have only zero in your checking account, you still don't have any money to truly live! In the same way, if all God did was put you and me at zero in our righteousness account, we couldn't truly live.

Here is the great news. We are more than forgiven! The resurrection of Jesus Christ makes us new creations who have been given the gift of righteousness! Romans 5:19 says, "Because one person disobeyed God, many became sinners. But because one other person obeyed God, many will be made righteous" (NLT). This clearly states that you, the sinner, were replaced with a new righteous you.

Some say God sees us only if we are righteous. No, we have become righteous in Christ. It's who we are. Let me say this directly to you: as a Christian, you have an account with God that declares you to be 100 percent righteous and makes your identity in Christ 100 percent righteousness!

Consider these questions: Can you do anything to increase your righteousness through obedience to God, pleasing God, good works, ministry, not sinning, and so on? Of course not. On the other hand, does sinning ever drop you below being 100 percent righteous? Again the good news is no. You are 100 percent righteous all the time, whether you obey or sin!

Isn't that great news? It's the understanding of this that makes the good news of the New Covenant as fantastic as God intended. No wonder Satan tries to keep it hidden from us.

Let's make this more personal by changing the word *righteousness* to the word *acceptable*. Have you ever thought that God only accepts you because he is kind and is God? He is both of those things, but that's not why he accepts you. He has a much better reason.

Before salvation, every person is 100 percent unacceptable to God. No one can change that through good works. After salvation, a Christian is 100 percent acceptable to God. That person cannot increase or decrease their acceptance with God, whether through obedience or sinning. We are unconditionally accepted by God because we are 100 percent acceptable to God by virtue of being 100 percent righteous in Christ.

That's why it's called grace! Doesn't that make you want to jump up and down and then fall on your knees and worship God?

You Cannot Mature Spiritually unless You Believe You Are Righteous

"I don't seem to be growing spiritually, and I can't figure out why," said Antoine. "My life as a Christian today seems no different from when I first believed in my early twenties. I've been involved in Bible studies, in men's groups, and I know a lot about Scripture. I occasionally fast and give financially to my local church. Plus, I've attempted to share the gospel with people God puts in my path.

"Yet I feel like something is missing. I've talked to my pastor and other spiritual mentors. They were sympathetic. But they mostly offered me books to read about discipleship and spiritual growth, which just seemed to put a different spin on everything I'm already doing."

Antoine's voice lowered. "I haven't told anybody else what I'm about to tell you, but I'm starting to feel worn down. I'm concerned that I may never grow spiritually and I'll forever feel stuck as a Christian."

Like Antoine, do you ever feel you are stuck in your spiritual growth? Have you tried different options to grow spiritually but still feel stagnant? Consider this perspective. Maybe the reason you feel stuck is that you've never really believed you are righteous.

I know that sounds like a bold statement. So first, let's make sure we understand the accurate definition of "spiritual growth." It's easy to think spiritual growth is only about increasing our understanding of Scripture, praying fervently for longer periods of time, and serving more effectively. These can certainly be some of the evidences and aids of spiritual growth, but I believe spiritual growth is much more. Spiritual growth (maturity) is living more and more like who we are in Christ, which is directly tied to the idea of our righteousness.

In Isaiah 61:3, God prophesied that the Messiah would fundamentally change who we are and that he would be glorified as a result. Look at what he says: "So they will be called oaks of righteousness, the planting of the LORD, that He may be glorified" (NASB).

In this verse, God calls us oaks of righteousness. When an oak tree first pushes through the ground as a seedling, it is 100 percent an oak tree already. For the remainder of its life, it will simply grow more and more into the oak tree it already is. In the same way, God wants you to understand that you're as righteous as you will ever be the moment you are saved. You and I will never be more righteous no matter how long we live. From that point until we die, however, we can grow more and more like who we already are as a righteous person in Christ.

That verse ends by saying that because God made us righteous, we can glorify him. The clear meaning is that because we are righteous in our identity in Christ, we can live like who we are. This is spiritual growth and spiritual maturity. This is what gives God glory.

What does giving God glory look like? It means we will think more and more like a righteous person. We will trust God in us more and more like a righteous person. We will act more and more like a righteous person. In other words, we will spiritually mature as a righteous person.

In contrast, one thing that can hinder spiritual growth is failing to believe we are righteous. Hebrews 5:13 says, "For everyone who partakes only of milk is not accustomed to the word of righteousness, for he is an infant" (NASB).

Our spiritual growth is compared to the growth of a person who by now should be a mature adult but is still an immature infant. Think about the picture being painted for us in this Scripture. If a three-month-old is drinking Mama's milk, that is adorable. But if a thirteen-year-old is drinking Mama's milk, that is weird! Yet many Christians are unaware that they are spiritually stunted and acting immature just like that thirteen-year-old.

Unless we have received very clear teaching that we are righteous and have embraced that truth by faith, it is impossible for us to fully mature in our spiritual lives. A spiritual ceiling we will never be able to break through looms over us until we are convinced we are righteous.

To be clear, this righteousness is our identity in Christ. It's who we are in the core of our being. It's who we are in our spirit. It's the essence of who we are as children of God. It's that oak of righteousness we are in Christ.

This Scripture is not saying we will live a perfectly righteous life. We will not. We will sin as long as we live on this earth. I will say, however, that in my many years of teaching these truths, I've watched numerous Christians progressively live a more righteous life. On the other hand, I've seen those who believe they are simply "sinners saved by grace" actually live a more sinful life. We truly do live our lives in a manner consistent with who we believe we are in our hearts.

Rest Occurs When You Know You're Unconditionally Accepted

In the world we live in, we work all day so we can rest at night. In God's kingdom, it's the opposite. We rest in Christ first so we can do good works second.

In Hebrews 4:9–10, we are told we as Christians have already entered into God's rest through our faith in Christ. "There remains, then, a Sabbath-rest for the people of God; for anyone who enters God's rest also rests from their works, just as God did from his."

To rest means to stop working completely. And the only way to experience the spiritual rest we have in Christ is to stop working or performing for God's acceptance because we know we are righteous in Christ. Until we do, we are deceived by a works-based righteousness. Most who do this are not working to get into heaven but are working to get God to love them, accept them, bless them, and use them more. The problem is that you never know when you've done enough, so you can never rest.

The only way to rest is to believe you are righteous. Only by doing that will you believe God accepts you because you are acceptable. That is what it means to enter into God's rest. It's to rest in the reality that you are righteous in Christ.

Do you read your Bible and pray so you can find inner rest? Do you serve God so you can rest? Do you obey God so you can rest? Do you attend church so you can find rest? I definitely encourage you to do those things, but from a place of rest, not to be at rest.

Sometimes when I'm feeling stressed, I pray, "Jesus, I am feeling really stressed out right now. I choose to sit down in you and rest." I do this by faith in my mind's eye because I know he is at rest.

Did you know that God rested two times? The first was after he completed his work of creation according to Genesis 2:2. The second was when Jesus sat down on his throne because he had completed the work of making us new creations according to verses such as Hebrews 1:3.

Jesus has done everything you and I need to be righteous and unconditionally accepted. In fact, he is our righteousness and more, according to 1 Corinthians 1:30: "By His doing you are in Christ Jesus, who became to us wisdom from God, and righteousness and sanctification, and redemption" (NASB).

This often seems to help my emotions calm down on the inside as I'm reminded that Jesus is my ultimate place of rest.

Let me say it again. The only way to rest is to believe that regardless of whether you feel righteous or have been behaving righteously, God has made you righteous and that is your true identity in Christ. Knowing you are righteous tells you that you are acceptable to God all day, every day. So relax. Rest in Christ and then let him live through you to do his work. It's one aspect of God's best-kept secret, for true inner rest.

Common Christian Distortions about Righteousness

After all you've read, you may still not believe you are righteous, and as a result, you may still disagree that you are unconditionally accepted by God. You may be close or even think you understand, but you may not be there yet.

For instance, you may believe God declares you are righteous because when he sees you he sees Jesus in you. So of course he says you are righteous. But that means God doesn't truly accept you; he just accepts Jesus on your behalf. But Jesus could not live in you if you were not as righteous as he is. Our righteous, holy God cannot coexist with sin. When God looks at you, he sees Jesus in you but he also sees you, the righteous new creation in Christ he made so he could live in you, and he is pleased.

There can be confusion about us having a robe of righteousness (see Isa. 61:10). Some erroneously believe this robe means God is covering us as sinners because he cannot stand to look at us. To the contrary, that robe is clothing that perfectly fits the righteous person you are in Christ.

You may believe in what some people call "positional" righteousness. In other words, God sees you *as if* you are righteous because he sees you as you *will be* in heaven one day, but you really aren't righteous now. What? Is God faking himself out, pretending you are somebody you really aren't? That's like saying that though the Bible describes our salvation as being born again, we weren't really born again. Is God just saying we were born again because that's what we will be in heaven? No, you are born again now and you are righteous now!

Maybe you've heard someone pray for God to hide them behind Jesus when they are about to sing, teach, or preach. I realize they want Jesus to be glorified in what they do, but to pray that prayer is a misunderstanding of the gospel. God doesn't need to hide you behind Jesus, because you are totally righteous. He likes seeing you directly.

Others confuse the gift of God's forgiveness with the gift of righteousness. They believe forgiveness is all they got and all they need, which somehow makes them righteous. Not at all. Forgiveness forever removes our unrighteousness only. We need the gift of righteousness to actually become righteous.

Second Corinthians 5:21 speaks to all these issues when it says, "God made him who had no sin to be sin for us, so that in him we might become the righteousness of God."

Astonishingly, we are told here that Christians have "become the righteousness of God." In other words, God gave us his own righteousness through our faith in Christ. That begs the question, How much of God's righteousness did we get? Did we get 50 percent? Or 75 percent? No, we received 100 percent of God's righteousness, which is now our righteousness in Christ.

At a conference where I was teaching these distortions, a pastor named Roy raised his hand and asked if he could say something. His comments were so profound that I've never forgotten them.

> As I listened to you teaching, I smugly believed I wasn't learning anything new. I thought I'd heard it all before. But then you completely messed me up when you went over those distortions we tend to believe about being righteous. Every one of them stabbed me like a knife and I realized how deceived I was. I really didn't believe I was righteous. I actually believed God just saw me that way. Now I can truly say with joy, "I knew I was saved but I didn't know I was *that* saved!"

Are you like Roy? Did you know you were saved but didn't know you were *that* saved? How awesome is our God and the salvation he has given us in Christ!

Because God made you righteous in Christ, you are unconditionally accepted by him and can't mess it up. He not only loves you; he likes you! This is the gospel not only for unbelievers but also for Christians, yet so few of them seem to have heard it.

Let's take this one step further. Because God accepts you, you can accept yourself. You may be wondering how you can accept yourself since you know how much you blow it and sin. The answer is this: if God accepts you, who are you to reject yourself?

Affirm Your Acceptance in Christ

As we conclude this chapter, would you like to pray right now and accept the reality that you are unconditionally acceptable to God? I invite you to believe God and to pray the following prayer by faith:

> *Father, when I examine my feelings and remember my failures, it doesn't seem true that I am righteous. Yet your Word tells me you have made me the righteousness of God in Christ. I now realize I have been trying to make myself more righteous so you would accept me more. I'm sorry I've done this. I realize this is error and sin. I agree with you right now that you have made me 100 percent righteous in my identity in Christ. I believe that because you gave me your righteousness, I am as righteous as you. I also choose to believe right now that you unconditionally accept me. And because you accept me, I choose to accept myself. Please make this more real to me day by day. In Jesus's name, Amen.*

In addition, consider this exercise to help you embrace this amazing truth for your own life. On a clean piece of paper, write these statements below:

Because you say I am righteous in Christ, I agree with you and say I am righteous in Christ.

Because you say I'm acceptable in Christ, I say I'm acceptable to you in Christ.

Because you accept me, I accept me.

And I can't mess any of this up!

Then tape the paper on your mirror and repeat this truth to yourself every day for the next thirty days. Believe this truth, repeat this truth, and watch it come alive in your life!

6

Christians Don't Need the Ten Commandments

When you look at the love story in the Bible that describes God creating Adam and Eve, do you notice he created them to live by grace through faith in him alone? But how do we know he created them to live this way?

We already saw that God intended to live in them. He also walked with them during the cool of the day. Because God walked with them and lived in them, heaven and earth coexisted—but that coexistence was based on love, not rules. Adam and Eve were satisfied completely with him and his love for them individually. They along with all of us were created to live a relationship-based existence with God, not a rule-based existence.

God's grace caused them to be created. They could not create themselves. God's grace resulted in God living in them. They could not have spiritual life within apart from God. They were the prototype of how a fully alive human is supposed to live—by grace through faith alone. They lived each day with a grace mentality.

God created you and saved you to live by grace through faith in him. He wants you to know the magnificent love he has for you as he lives in you. He wants you to be satisfied with his love. He wants you to trust him and obey him, not out of obligation, but as an expression of your love for him. When you know you are loved so deeply, it's a normal response to love God like this. This kind of love for God is not a guilt-motivated obligation. It is a gratitude-motivated free choice. He wants you to live with a grace mentality.

God Does Not Bless Christians because They Obey Rules

Although God never intended for us to live by laws, once the knowledge of good and evil became Adam and Eve's core belief system, that all changed. The knowledge that entered them was the beginning of living by law. It changed their entire approach to God and life. They went from a grace mentality to a law mentality. We all inherited this law mentality from them. Once the human race began to think this way, God seemed to say, "If you want to live by laws, I will give you the ultimate laws to live by. I will give you the Ten Commandments along with 613 other commandments. These will be absolute unchangeable laws, based not on faulty human standards but on my perfect character."

He did this with a specific group of people called the nation of Israel, whom he planned to use to reveal himself as the only true God to all the other nations of the earth at that time. Through Moses he then asked the people if they wanted to enter into this kind of relationship with him, a covenant relationship:

> If you obey me fully and keep my covenant, then out of all nations you will be my treasured possession. Although the whole earth is mine, you will be for me a kingdom of priests and a holy nation. (Exod. 19:5–6)

It was not a question to be taken lightly. They were being asked to enter into a relationship that would later be called the Old Covenant. A covenant is like nothing we have today in our culture. At that time, a covenant might be an agreement between a conquering king and the conquered people. Or two equal parties. A covenant was unbreakable as long as either party was alive.

Though he was their God and King, he asked them if they were willing to enter into a covenant relationship. In Exodus, we see this entire story played out and Israel agreeing to do it.

These adults, however, all died in the wilderness, and then God asked their adult children if they would agree to this same covenant. There was one condition to the Old Covenant for Israel—obedience. Look at what he says to them in Deuteronomy 28:1–2:

> Now it shall be, if you diligently obey the LORD your God, being careful to do all His commandments which I command you today, the LORD your God will set you high above all the nations of the earth. All these blessings will come upon you and overtake you if you obey the LORD your God. (NASB)

The next twelve verses list all the blessings God would give to Israel if they obeyed his commandments in this covenant. In verse 15, however, God also tells them if they didn't obey the covenant, they would be cursed: "It shall come about, if you do not obey the LORD your God, to observe to do all His commandments and His statutes with which I charge you today, that all these curses will come upon you and overtake you" (NASB).

Now here comes the shock! Over fifty verses explain curses God promises would come on Israel if they didn't obey his commandments! This is four times as many curses as blessings in the Old Covenant.

Do you want to live under that arrangement with God? I certainly don't, but a lot of Christians do without realizing it. If you believe you should obey the Ten Commandments or any of the Old Covenant commandments, you are saying you do.

Some Christians don't necessarily try to keep the Ten Commandments, but they still believe God will bless them if they obey him and curse (or punish) them if they don't obey him. In either case, these are New Covenant Christians with an Old Covenant mind-set.

The main purpose of the Ten Commandments and the 613 other commandments was not to bless people. It was to show people their sins and prepare them for a savior. Romans 3:20 and Galatians 3:22 show us this. (The bracketed insertion is mine to bring clarity.)

> No one will be declared righteous in God's sight by the works of the law; rather, through the law we become conscious of our sin.

> The [Old Testament] Scriptures declare that we are all prisoners of sin, so we receive God's promise of freedom only by believing in Jesus Christ. (NLT)

The New Covenant Is Superior to the Old Covenant

To completely let go of the Old Covenant, it's essential that you understand the New Covenant. While this entire book is an explanation of the New Covenant, let's focus on what I mentioned briefly in chapter 2. Scripture teaches us about three pillars in the New Covenant, but first and foremost, it tells us Jesus Christ is the foundation upon which each of these three pillars rests.

Ironically, an Old Testament prophecy that is repeated in Hebrews 10:16–17 gives the most succinct description of the New Covenant. In Jeremiah 31:31–34, we read,

> "Behold, days are coming," declares the LORD, "when I will make a new covenant with the house of Israel and with the house of Judah, not like the covenant which I made with their fathers in the day I took them by the hand to bring them out of the land of Egypt, My covenant which they broke, although I was a husband to them,"

declares the LORD. "But this is the covenant which I will make with the house of Israel after those days," declares the LORD, "I will put My law within them and on their heart I will write it; and I will be their God, and they shall be My people. They will not teach again, each man his neighbor and each man his brother, saying, 'Know the LORD,' for they will all know Me, from the least of them to the greatest of them," declares the LORD, "for I will forgive their iniquity, and their sin I will remember no more." (NASB)

This was written to God's Jewish people many years after the Old Covenant was instituted. No one knew this prophecy would include the Gentiles—non-Jews. God tells us in verse 32 that the New Covenant would not be like the Old Covenant; it would be very different. The big takeaway from that is that the Old Covenant was temporary and external and didn't work. The New Covenant is eternal and internal and does work.

Here are the three pillars from Jeremiah 31:

1. Who we are in Christ
   Verse 33 says God is going to write his law on our hearts. In the Old Covenant, God's law was written on two stone slabs of rock. In the New Covenant, God writes his law on our hearts, meaning his character is placed in our hearts. This is our new heart in Christ. It is why we are as righteous as Jesus. It's why we are saints and much more. It's why we don't need the external law of the Old Covenant. It's why we're no longer dead but are alive in Christ!

2. Who Christ is in us
   The next verse, 34, says we will not have to tell Christians to know the Lord because every one of us will know him. The Hebrew word for "know" here means union, just as it does in Genesis 4:1: "Adam knew Eve his wife, and she conceived and bore Cain, and said, 'I have acquired a man from the

LORD'" (NKJV). What God is saying to us is that in the Old Covenant, the Jewish people were constantly telling people to do something impossible—to have a close, intimate relationship with God. When the High Priest represented them in the Holy of Holies was as close to God as they could ever get. In the New Covenant, God changed this by spiritually uniting himself to us. This union means we are always close to God and can never get any closer. We may feel closer to God at times, but we can't get closer. It also means we can enjoy intimacy with him 24/7.

3. Our eternal, complete forgiveness

Verse 34 also gives us the great news that through the sacrifice of Jesus Christ, our sins are so forgiven that God doesn't remember them—ever. This means he never holds them against us because we are forgiven for every sin—past, present, and future—from the moment of our salvation. That is such a dramatic contrast with Old Covenant forgiveness. All those sacrifices each year were never enough to forgive their past sins and certainly not their future sins.

Read those verses one more time while you ask yourself one question: What is God's part in the New Covenant and what is your part?

You didn't find your part because it's not there. God does his part *and* he does *your* part! God made a covenant with himself and we are the beneficiaries. In the Old Covenant, God did his part and the Jews were to do their part. God was faithful to keep his part but the Jews were most often unfaithful because they were sinners in their hearts. The external law of God couldn't change that. The New Covenant, however, took care of our problem internally by giving us a new heart in Christ.

We are to "do" only one thing in the New Covenant: simply believe. Just as obedience was the condition in the Old Covenant, faith is the condition in the New Covenant. In other words, we are to believe for our salvation and we are to live by faith from then on, relying on Christ in us.

Great blessings are in the New Covenant. Ephesians 1:3 says we already have them just because we are Christians: "Blessed be the God and Father of our Lord Jesus Christ, who has blessed us with every spiritual blessing in the heavenly places in Christ" (NASB).

Where are these blessings? They are in Christ, which is where you are today. The blessings, however, will not do you a lot of good in daily life if you don't believe. For example, God unconditionally accepts you as one of those blessings. Yet you can enjoy this only if you believe it is true every day. That is why it is so important to tell God you believe these blessings are true for you. Why don't you start right now by praying, "Father, I believe by faith that you unconditionally accept me today."

Obedience to God is still important. But as Christians living under the New Covenant, we obey God by faith because we are *already* blessed, not to get blessed.

Christians Have Something Better than Living by Rules

I have some great news for you. The New Covenant says you died on the cross with Christ to all religious rule-keeping, including the law. God removed from you all obligation to obey the law in the Old Covenant and exchanged it for a love relationship with Jesus Christ through his New Covenant. Romans 7:4 says, "My brothers and sisters, you also died to the law through the body of Christ, that you might belong to another, to him who was raised from the dead, in order that we might bear fruit for God."

Some believe our death to the law and our freedom from it applies only to our justification but not our sanctification. That is a huge stretch. If we died to the law, we died permanently to the law. Similarly, if we were released from the law as Romans 7:6 says, then we were released from the law permanently.

> By dying to what once bound us, we have been released from the law so that we serve in the new way of the Spirit, and not in the old way of the written code.

Galatians 3:25–26 shows us this same truth:

> Now that this faith has come, we are no longer under a guardian. So in Christ Jesus you are all children of God through faith.

Could this be any clearer? Once we come to faith in Jesus Christ, we don't need the guardian any longer, meaning we don't need the law. Do you know why? It's because we have something much better. First, as we saw in pillar one above, God has written the law on our hearts. Let me be clear. God did not write the Ten Commandments on our hearts. Since the Ten Commandments are based on the character of God, it means he placed his character in our hearts. This is our identity in Christ. It's what 2 Peter 1:4 means when it says, "Through these he has given us his very great and precious promises, so that through them you may participate in the divine nature, having escaped the corruption in the world caused by evil desires."

Second, we have the Holy Spirit in us to fill us with the life of Christ so he can live through us. The law says try harder. Grace says trust more. If you don't believe this, you will burn out on the Christian life over and over. If you do believe this, you will learn to rest in Christ as he does the work through you more and more.

Did you know that if you go back to the Ten Commandments as a Christian, you are committing spiritual adultery? That is exactly what Romans 7:4 told us earlier.

Our spiritual adultery of trying to keep the law also keeps us in bondage by making Christianity a heavy, exhausting burden instead of the joyful, abundant life it is meant to be.

Have you had enough of trying to live by the Ten Commandments and religious rules? If so, it's time to start living by the dynamic, life-giving power of God's grace, which will lead you into freedom.

Here is something you can do to apply this to your life today. Do it as you are driving to or from work. Or if you are home waiting for your family to arrive. Rehearse why you have something so much better than the law to live from. Confess this out loud:

I have something amazingly better than the law or religious rules to live from today. I have my new identity in Christ. I have Jesus Christ in me to love me and to live the Christian life through me. I am going to live by grace through faith today because of these New Covenant truths.

What Do You Follow?

Ice cream comes in many flavors, but regardless of the taste, it's still ice cream. In the same way, legalistic religious rules based on denomination or personal preferences have many different flavors, but no matter the type, they are still religious rules.

Here's an exercise to help identify when you might be living by religious rules. Consider these ideas to be like a warning light on your car's dashboard telling you something is wrong with your vehicle.

1. *You feel afraid of God's punishment.*

   When you fear God's punishment, tell him you remember you are no longer under law, but under grace. Thank him that he loves you and is not going to punish those he loves.

2. *You feel condemned.*

   You can spot that feeling of condemnation by remembering that condemnation always attacks your identity. You get messages that something is wrong with you as a Christian because of some far past or recent failure. When that happens, stop and pray, asking God to show you what religious rule you are living under. Then remember being under grace is being under no condemnation (Rom. 8:1).

3. *You find yourself thinking, "I should be doing* _____ " *(fill in the blank).*

Using the word *should* is almost always about obligation. It's a strong sense of duty that feels like a burden. When this happens, tell God your only obligation is to Jesus and not to any kind of "should." I once heard of a woman who placed a banner behind her desk that said, "Thou shalt not should on thyself today!"

4. *You believe perfection must be the goal and any mistake is a failure.*

This belief is usually about self-acceptance. It means you have yourself under some kind of religious rule that you have to do everything perfectly. You don't. When you see this in your life, tell God that you realize you are free to make mistakes. You don't have to do everything right or perfect, because you are under grace.

How do you break the pattern of living under self-imposed religious rules? The answer may feel wrong at first, but here's the best course of action to break the stranglehold on your life. When you identify a rule you put on yourself, make a conscious effort to "skip it." For example, based on the list above,

- Skip reading your Bible for a week and instead do an activity you really enjoy.
- Skip church attendance one week to spend genuine quality time with your family.
- Skip giving money to your church one week and give it to someone else God shows you who is in need.

- Skip being nice to someone for the sake of trying to get good karma.
- Skip thinking that God will punish you for skipping the activities on this list!

Skip following your religious rules and do something that makes you feel free. For instance, instead of praying before a meal, tell the people with you that God knows you're thankful and enjoy eating. Read a book not specifically Christian. Listen to music that is not Christian music for a week. Go to a movie you are interested in and see if God might speak to you through it.

I must warn you, however, to be prepared for the false guilt Satan (and other people) will try to make you feel when you decide to skip a religious rule. Satan will try to make you think the guilt is from God. Stand against this lie. Don't give in to it. Talk to God and remind yourself that you died with Christ to the law, including all religious rules and every kind of law-based mentality. You are now under grace instead. It may take awhile to get used to the feeling of freedom, but you can do it through Christ in you!

When God first revealed to me this liberating part of the New Covenant, I spent a few days struggling with some anxiety. This thought would go through my mind: *Maybe I should just go back to the way I used to live under religious rules. It feels more godly.* But in those moments I remembered how living by religious rules had almost destroyed me—producing inner struggles and an inability to love as a result of stunting my spiritual growth. Since then I've never entertained the idea of going back.

Living by Rules Won't Help You Grow Spiritually

Neither religious rules nor the Ten Commandments will help you grow spiritually. That's right; those rules have no ability to guide you into living a holy life. In fact, if you look closely, they tell only what you should *not* do.

The main way to grow spiritually is to live intimately with God from our union with Christ and focus on who we are in Christ. This is the true life of grace. This is growing in the grace and knowledge of our Lord and Savior Jesus Christ. As 2 Peter 3:18 says, "Grow in the grace and knowledge of our Lord and Savior Jesus Christ. To him be glory both now and forever! Amen."

A man named George once said to me after I spoke at the worship service at his church, "I can hardly believe it, but God's truth has been right here in front of my nose. Romans 7:1–4 says I died with Christ on the cross to any obligation to keep the Ten Commandments. My relationship is with Jesus alone and not the law. No wonder my relationship with God has become stale. I want to live by grace now. But I'm still confused. Do I just sit around and wait for God to do something to me?"

"In one sense, that is true, George," I told him. "Maturing in Christ is based on what God has already done for you and to you. That means living the same way Jesus lived. Remember how I taught from Scripture today how Jesus lived fully human as a man, though he was also God? The way he lived was by faith, dependent on his Father, who lived in him. In the same way, God wants you to live by faith, dependent on Christ in you. He is your only source for spiritual maturity. The more you depend on him, the more you will mature."

I continued, "This also includes reminding yourself over and over of the truth about your identity in Christ. The more you remember that truth, the more you will mature. So here is what I would suggest for you. Spend time talking with God, daily telling him that you are relying on Jesus in you to live through you in every area of your life—in your job, being a husband and a dad, with your eating, and so on. Also, when you talk with him, tell him you believe who he tells you that you are in Christ—righteous, holy,

Christians Don't Need the Ten Commandments

good, patient, and all those other truths based on the Scriptures I gave you. Then let's watch what God does in your life."

The next time I saw George he was beaming and said, "Mark, I'm amazed at what God has done in my life. The more I rely on Jesus in me and tell God how much I believe my identity in Christ, the more I sense God's love for me. What is really cool is that I love God more than I ever have. I love my wife and children more than I ever have. I want to be with them, whereas before I didn't care that much about them. Even my boss has asked me what has happened to me. He says I seem more motivated at work, and we've had some really challenging projects. I really am maturing in Christ. Thank you so much for sharing with me my freedom from the law and how to live by grace!"

Freedom from the Law Is Not Hyper-Grace

Some people believe Christians who think they're free from the law or religious rules are guilty of what's called "hyper-grace." The term means someone who isn't serious about obeying God and believes they have a license to sin. By license, I mean they believe God no longer cares whether they sin because they are under grace. Some can take this to an even further extreme and say that because of grace there is no such thing as sin. Both of these beliefs are incorrect.

My experience counseling and teaching thousands of Christians reveals just the opposite. Those who embrace God's grace sin a whole lot less than those who don't. They also obey God a whole lot more than those who don't. They will not live a sinless lifestyle, but they will sin less. On the other hand, I've seen that legalistic, rule-based Christians don't lead lifestyles as holy as they claim. They sin more, just usually behind closed doors.

Christians who embrace God's grace not only sin less, but because they live under grace, they love more. Their freedom from sin's power and the law's obligation enables them to love in a way they never have been able to do before. That was certainly true for me.

Did you know a genuine holy lifestyle is a life of love? A life of love is simply our Holy God, who is love, expressing himself through us. When this is occurring, guess what is happening. Christians are fulfilling the law without even thinking about the law. They are thinking about loving people. Romans 13:10 says it this way: "Love does no harm to a neighbor. Therefore love is the fulfillment of the law."

That's why true grace will never lead you into the errors of disobedience and taking sin lightly. Once you fall into any of these deceptions from Satan, you are not living by grace. You are living according to the flesh.

Three responses to God's grace are always possible for Christians:

1. *Refuse God's grace*—rejecting the teaching they need to live by grace and making the law and trying harder the focal point of their Christian lives.

2. *Abuse God's grace*—taking God's grace and perverting it, diminishing sin and disobedience to the point that they think God is okay with it.

3. *Use God's grace*—understanding the truth, that the only way to live the Christian life victoriously is to live it by grace.

One of my favorite passages on this subject is Titus 2:11–12, which says, "The grace of God has appeared that offers salvation to all people. It teaches us to say 'No' to ungodliness and worldly passions, and to live self-controlled, upright and godly lives in this present age."

God's grace teaches some to "unlearn" legalism. God's grace teaches others to "unlearn" worldliness.

Grace Is a Person

As we conclude this chapter, please realize that grace is a Person. Jesus Christ is the embodiment of grace. To live by grace is to live by him and all that he is.

Because Jesus Christ is "Mr. Grace," the Bible communicates that Christians are the bride of Christ and the body of Christ (Eph. 5:32; 1 Cor. 12:27). We are the bride of Christ for the purpose of intimacy with Jesus in us. We are the body of Christ for the purpose of Jesus doing his ministry through us on this earth.

Let today be a new beginning for you to live as the bride and body of Christ, because you are free from religious rules.

Let today be a new beginning for you to live free from religious rules. Take a step of faith and pray this prayer to let go of trying to live by the law, and to live by God's grace:

> *Dear Father, I admit that I have not understood that I have something better than the Ten Commandments or religious rules to live by. I realize that I have been living from a law mentality instead of a grace mentality. I'm very sorry, and I give up on trying to get you to help me try harder. I embrace my identity in Christ and Christ in me in place of the law. I want to live by grace from this time forward. I look forward to living in the freedom from the law and sin you gave me when I was crucified and raised with Christ. I also look forward to the freedom to love you, myself, and other people. Amen.*

I hope you see that living by grace through faith is one aspect of the secret every Christian is dying to know. As the Holy Spirit leads, let's lovingly and graciously share this truth with the Christians God puts in our paths.

7

Christians Are Forgiven before They Ever Sin

Pick your favorite sin. When I say "favorite," I mean a sin you keep committing over and over, more than any other. In other words, what is the sin you hate but can't seem to stop doing? Or what is a sinful habit you've tried to stop without success?

Now imagine that you just committed that sin again for the millionth time. Do you think in God's eyes you are forgiven? Or do you think he looks at you with contempt and frustration? Do you wonder if God gets so tired of you committing the same sin that you can go too far and break fellowship with him?

When you can't stop sinning, do you think you have to prove to God how sorry you are to get his forgiveness? Or do you struggle to pray the right prayer or say the right words so God will forgive you?

Here's part of the best-kept secret about being a Christian: Forgiveness from God isn't based on what you do. Forgiveness is based on what God has already done for you. The problem is if you get this concept mixed up, you can live in bondage to unnecessary guilt.

Chang was a Christian friend I met in college at a campus ministry we both attended. The focus of the group was to train students in personal evangelism and how to grow spiritually. One of the Bible verses the ministry leader stressed, however, was 1 John 1:9, which says, "If we confess our sins, He is faithful and just to forgive us our sins and to cleanse us from all unrighteousness" (NKJV).

Our group leader would emphasize that if we confess our sins to God and ask him to forgive us each time, we can be certain we're forgiven. But if we didn't confess, we wouldn't be forgiven and would lose fellowship with God. In essence, a spiritual barrier would come between us and God. As long as the barrier was there, God could not hear our prayers. The ministry leader also quoted Psalm 66:18, which says, "If I regard iniquity in my heart, the Lord will not hear" (NKJV).

Chang said to me, "No wonder God doesn't seem to answer my prayers sometimes. I guess he couldn't hear me because I had sin in my life that I hadn't confessed and asked forgiveness for."

"I feel the same way you do, Chang," I said. "I think this principle will help make us both better Christians, don't you?"

Chang said, "What if I sin but forget to confess it to God and ask for forgiveness? I wouldn't avoid it on purpose, but what if I get busy and just forget? It seems like you could get out of fellowship with God for days and not even know it."

After our discussion, I noticed a strange thing started to happen to Chang over the next few months. When we first met, he'd been a happy, vibrant guy everyone liked. But he slowly began to drift into a serious state of mind. By the end of the school year, Chang was flat-out depressed.

Between classes one day, I bumped into him and saw dark circles under his eyes. I said, "Chang, you don't look so good. Is there anything I can do to help?"

Chang replied, "Do you remember when we met earlier and talked about confessing our sins to God? I realized I wasn't keeping my sin account with God up-to-date. I've tried to keep confessing my sins to God as 1 John 1:9 tells us, but it seems like the more I focus on doing this, the more my joy in the Lord is leaving me. I guess now that you mention it, I do feel depressed and a little fearful. I'm walking around every day feeling afraid that I'm going to get out of fellowship with God if I don't confess every little sin." Then we had to leave for our next class.

Sadly, that was the last time I ever saw Chang. He didn't return to college the next year, and I suspect his spiritual struggles were a contributing factor.

Neither Chang nor I realized at the time that 1 John 1:9 and much of the remainder of the letter was written to Christians warning them about a group infiltrating the church that was just beginning. Later, their teaching would become Gnosticism, which believed weird stuff like Jesus was only spiritual and did not have a real body. They also believed they were sinless. John was addressing both of those heresies, saying that confessing sin is an admission that a person is a sinner in need of salvation. It's not a verse for people after they become Christians.

We also didn't realize Christians cannot break fellowship with God or have a barrier between them and God when they sin. Both are impossible because they are in an unbreakable union with God.

Christians Don't Need More Forgiveness

Here's the real truth about God's forgiveness: When you place your faith in Jesus Christ, you never need to try to get more of his forgiveness. You already have all the forgiveness you will ever need for every sin before you ever commit it! The Bible makes this truth quite clear. Ephesians 1:7 says, "In him we have redemption through his blood, the forgiveness of sins, in accordance with the riches of God's grace."

If you want to live according to God's best-kept secret, pay close attention to all the riches you already have. In addition to the complete forgiveness you have in Christ, you are already holy and blameless before God, as well as adopted sons and daughters. These, too, are great blessings we already have in Christ.

> He chose us in him before the creation of the world to be holy and blameless in his sight. In love he predestined us for adoption to sonship through Jesus Christ, in accordance with his pleasure and will—to the praise of his glorious grace, which he has freely given. (Eph. 1:4–6)

Don't miss the point that you already have all these blessings, including the blessing of complete forgiveness. Where is your forgiveness found? In Christ. Where are you today as a follower of Jesus? In Christ! This means each time you sin, whether or not you know you have sinned, you are in Christ, surrounded by all the forgiveness you will ever need. Colossians 2:13–14 states this amazing truth in a different way:

> When you were dead in your sins and in the uncircumcision of your flesh, God made you alive with Christ. He forgave us all our sins, having canceled the charge of our legal indebtedness, which stood against us and condemned us; he has taken it away, nailing it to the cross.

Do you see the point God is making? God forgave you for *all* your sins. Not just the past ones before your salvation, but also the present ones, and even the future sins. Do you wonder how he could forgive your future sins when you haven't even committed them yet? Well, weren't they all in the future when Jesus died on the cross?

Colossians 2:14 goes on to tell us that God canceled the legal debt we owed him. This debt is what condemned you as guilty and worthy of death and hell. This legal debt is your list of all the sins you will ever commit from the time you are born to the time you die. That great number of sins has been nailed to the cross of Jesus! When he cried out "It is finished!" and then died, that debt was completely removed forever.

If you still aren't convinced that you are 100 percent forgiven for your sins—past, present, and future—let's look at Hebrews 10:17–18: "Their sins and lawless acts I will remember no more. And where these have been forgiven, sacrifice for sin is no longer necessary."

First, we are so forgiven that God doesn't remember our sins. The death of Jesus has taken care of each one. Second, he's telling us that once we have complete forgiveness through Jesus's sacrifice on the cross, no other sacrifice is needed. To the Jews, this would have been difficult to believe. They had been going to the temple for thousands of years to present sacrifices for their sins. Similarly, it's difficult for Christians today to believe God has forgiven them for their present and future sins.

God Is Not Waiting for You to Ask for Forgiveness

For many years I beat myself up with tremendous guilt whenever I sinned. This self-imposed guilt sometimes led to deep self-loathing. In my counseling experience, I have found that many Christians beat themselves up just as I did, and maybe you wrestle with this very problem today.

Here's the way I used to struggle.

Earlier in my life, I had only a partial understanding of my forgiveness as a Christian, and I didn't quite know what to do when I sinned. For example, in college one of my friends, Gary, started dating a girl right after I broke up with her. Her name was Andrea. I was livid with Gary. I got so angry that I couldn't sleep. I'd wake up and walk around campus in the middle of the night, boiling with inner rage.

113

As my anger continued, the Lord began to show me I was sinning. I had no right to ask Gary not to date Andrea. She was no longer my girlfriend. I had become angry because I believed I had the right to his loyalty.

When God showed me this attitude, I thought, *I need to ask God to forgive me and to show him how sorry I really am for my sins of anger and bitterness. If I feel guilty long enough, I'm sure he will forgive me completely and I will be back in fellowship with him.*

I continued to beat myself up for days, repeating, *I'm such a failure as a Christian. Look at how long I allowed that anger and bitterness to control me. God must be disappointed with me.*

I didn't realize there was no need for me to ask for forgiveness and certainly no need to beat myself up. God doesn't want any of his children to hate themselves when they sin. We don't need to prove to God how sorry we are. God wants us to talk with him when we sin, confident that he has already forgiven us.

Because I now understand this gospel called the New Covenant, my response when I sin is very different from what it used to be. I certainly tell God I'm sorry when he shows me I've sinned, yet I do it not hoping I'll get more forgiveness. I do it with a confident belief that I am already forgiven because I am in Christ. This strengthens the peace I have underneath the sadness I feel. This sadness is because I did not act like who I am in Christ, a child of my Father. I know that grieves the Holy Spirit, meaning he feels sad but not mad. We see this in Ephesians 4:30, which says, "Do not grieve the Holy Spirit of God, with whom you were sealed for the day of redemption" (NASB).

After I tell God I'm sorry, I thank him that Jesus died for that sin and that I am forgiven. Then I repent, which means in the Greek language to change your mind. This does not mean I commit myself to try harder not to do that sin again. That never works. It means I realize I cannot stop myself from doing this sin again—no matter how many times I read about it in Scripture, pray, or ask others to pray for me.

I repent by turning to Jesus, asking him to show me why I sinned. It is often because I was looking to meet one of my God-given needs—such as love, acceptance, or worth—through the flesh. As he shows me why I did what I did, I ask him to remind me that those needs are met in him. I ask him to handle the problem through me next time I'm tempted. Using anger as an example, here is a typical prayer I say to God:

> *Father, I am sorry I committed the sin of anger. I know that as your son, I am not an angry person in Christ, but I've just acted the opposite. I have lived according to the flesh instead of the Spirit. I thank you that you forgave me for this sin when Jesus died on the cross. I now repent by turning to Jesus in me. Jesus, I ask you to show me why I got angry. I also ask you to live through me so I will not sin with this kind of anger again. Amen.*

Will God Forgive Us If We Don't Forgive?

Some Christians are confused about whether God will forgive us if we don't forgive. This appears to come mainly from the Lord's Prayer because one part seems to contradict the idea that we are already forgiven for all our sins. The Lord's Prayer is found in Matthew 6:10–13, and verse 12 says, "Forgive us our debts [our sins], as we also have forgiven our debtors [those who have sinned against us]" (NASB, bracketed words mine).

How do we deal with this?

In this prayer, Jesus mentions two conditions for being forgiven. The first is that to get God's forgiveness we must ask for it. The second is that we must forgive people to get God's forgiveness.

Some say we should pray the Lord's Prayer because Jesus taught it. But if you are going to use that reasoning, you need to apply that to other things he taught.

For example, in Matthew 5:28 Jesus says, "Anyone who looks at a woman lustfully has already committed adultery with her in his heart." Jesus goes on to say that if someone has had sexual thoughts about anyone other than their spouse, that person should pluck out an eye to avoid going to hell! Maybe you're skeptical, thinking, *Jesus is speaking in hyperbole. He didn't really mean that. He was just trying to make a point.* I agree that he was trying to make a point, but his point was not hyperbole. He was teaching that the Ten Commandments, including the seventh commandment about avoiding adultery, are not just about what you do. It's also about what you think. He was raising the standard for what sin really is. He was showing how sinful people are.

We need to think not only about what Jesus was teaching but to whom he was teaching. Do you realize the ministry of Jesus in Matthew, Mark, Luke, and John—even to his Jewish disciples— was a ministry to those under the Old Covenant? This means most of what Jesus taught during his time on earth was to Jewish people under the law. Some things he taught weren't—like being born again in John 3, confronting those who sin against you in Matthew 18, and abiding in Christ in John 15—but the majority were. Jesus was preparing these Jews to see how sinful they were so he could be their only means of salvation. Today, any Jew or non-Jew who reads the Gospels will hopefully be convinced of their own sinfulness so they, too, can be saved.

As Christians, we need to understand this about Jesus's teaching. Then we can read the Gospels of Matthew, Mark, Luke, and John through a New Covenant lens, applying it with clearer understanding.

When Jesus Christ died, was buried, and rose again, everything changed. The New Covenant replaced the Old Covenant. Hebrews

8:13 expresses it this way: "By calling this covenant 'new,' he has made the first one obsolete; and what is obsolete and outdated will soon disappear."

This is critical for us to understand. This created a fundamental change in how God relates to us and how we can relate to him, including how God forgives us.

We've already seen from verses like Colossians 2:13–14 and Ephesians 1:7 that we have complete forgiveness because we are in Christ. Those Jewish disciples whom Jesus taught the Lord's Prayer were not in him yet.

Paul wrote in Ephesians 4:32, "Be kind and compassionate to one another, forgiving each other, just as in Christ God forgave you." This says the exact opposite of the Lord's Prayer. It tells us to forgive *because* we are already forgiven in Christ. This is after the cross when the New Covenant had been put in place by Jesus's death and resurrection. That's one reason the New Covenant is amazingly better than the Old Covenant.

You Cannot Out-Sin God's Grace

As a Christian, you are completely forgiven for sins you know about and don't know about. No matter how much you ever sin, you will never be able to out-sin God's grace. In other words, no magic number of sins will be so great that God has not already forgiven you for them. Also, no specific type of sin is so terrible that God has not already forgiven it.

Do you realize not one sin you will ever commit will catch God by surprise? He's never going to turn to the angels when you sin and say, "Oh no! I forgot to put that one on the cross when Jesus died! I guess this one will have to go to hell!"

You cannot out-sin God's grace! His grace will always exceed your sins. Always. If you are having a difficult time believing me, let's take a look at Romans 5:20: "The law was brought in so that the trespass might increase. But where sin increased, grace increased all the more."

Do you see the last part of that verse? "Where sin increased, grace increased all the more." Personalize that verse. Use your name below and say this out loud three times:

Where [your name]'s sin increased, God's grace increased all the more.

Think about the worst sin you have ever committed in your life. Then insert it in that phrase again and repeat it out loud, preferably where no one can hear you.

Where [your name]'s sin of [name it] increased, God's grace increased all the more.

This doesn't mean natural consequences never occur because of our sins. They do. If you rob a bank, God will have already forgiven you, but you still go to jail.

Many people fear teaching people they are already forgiven before they sin will lead them to go wild and sin all they can. I mean, why not? If we are already forgiven before we sin, let's just go out and sin, sin, sin! What is there to keep us from sinning if we are forgiven for even our future sins, right?

First, to struggle with that question is not necessarily bad. When Christians realize the reality of God's amazing grace in the New Covenant in all its glory, that should cause some to ask, "Are you saying it's okay to sin because God won't care?" In fact, that's a good test as to what we are being taught about true grace from the Bible.

What, then, is the answer to this valid question? Does God need to give people some laws so they won't sin? Not at all. God anticipated us questioning whether it might be okay to sin because all our sins have already been forgiven. He gave the answer in Romans

6:1–2: "What shall we say then? Are we to continue in sin so that grace may increase? May it never be! How shall we who died to sin still live in it?" (NASB).

God's answer is that each of us died to sin as the ruling power over our lives. This happened to you and me when we died with Jesus Christ on the cross and rose with him as new creations. Your new identity in Christ is righteous and loves righteousness, not sinning. The real you doesn't want to sin. You want to live a righteous lifestyle more than your flesh wants to sin. As a saint, a holy person, you don't want to sin. It's contrary to your nature. You want to live a holy lifestyle. I don't mean a rule-based, checklist-based, legalistic lifestyle, but a lifestyle the opposite of sinning.

God Does Not Get Angry with You When You Sin

As I think about the amazing forgiveness God has provided for us, I think of a song I used to sing when I went to a Bible study with several hundred other college students. The chorus says,

> He paid a debt he did not owe.
> I owed a debt I could not pay.
> I needed someone to wash my sins away.
> And now I sing a brand-new song, "Amazing Grace."
> Christ Jesus paid a debt that I could never pay.
>
> Ellis J. Crum,
> "He Paid a Debt He Did Not Owe"

The words in this song tell us in wonderful rhyme that as Christians, we have no legal guilt before God that would cause him to condemn us. That is why when bad things happen to us, any thought that God is punishing us is from Satan. It is never from God.

Let me put it another way, and please read this slowly. God's problem with your sins has been dealt with forever! He has removed the guilt of our sins forever, both the legal guilt and even the emotional guilt.

Though we have no guilt before God, we will feel godly sorrow when God shows us we have sinned, according to 2 Corinthians 7:10: "Godly sorrow brings repentance that leads to salvation and leaves no regret, but worldly sorrow brings death."

This sorrow is what leads us to repent, as mentioned earlier.

The Difference between God's Punishment and His Discipline

That brings us to the big difference between God's punishment and God's discipline. There is no punishment from God for believers. God no longer needs to punish you for any sin. Jesus Christ took your punishment for every one of your sins. All the punishment you deserve for your sins is complete! In addition, 1 John 2:2 says, "He Himself is the propitiation for our sins; and not for ours only, but also for those of the whole world" (NASB).

How long has it been since you thanked God for your propitiation? The word *propitiation* means God's anger because of your sin was completely satisfied and removed when Jesus died in your place on the cross. He is never going to get angry with you and punish you for a sin.

In contrast, God does discipline us—because he loves us, not because he is angry with us. His discipline is meant to help us when we've gotten off track and not lived like his child. Like any good father, he wants to help get us back on track. Hebrews 12:4–11 tells us,

> In your struggle against sin, you have not yet resisted to the point of shedding your blood. And have you completely forgotten this word of encouragement that addresses you as a father addresses his son? It says, "My son, do not make light of the Lord's discipline, and do not lose heart when he rebukes you, because the Lord disciplines the one he loves, and he chastens everyone he accepts as his son."

Endure hardship as discipline; God is treating you as his children. For what children are not disciplined by their father? If you are not disciplined—and everyone undergoes discipline—then you are not legitimate, not true sons and daughters at all. Moreover, we have all had human fathers who disciplined us and we respected them for it. How much more should we submit to the Father of spirits and live! They disciplined us for a little while as they thought best; but God disciplines us for our good, in order that we may share in his holiness. No discipline seems pleasant at the time, but painful. Later on, however, it produces a harvest of righteousness and peace for those who have been trained by it.

You can see that God's discipline proves we are one of his children and that he loves us. We also see that he disciplines us so we can "share in his holiness." When we rely on our Holy God, with whom we are united, his holiness can flow through us. Then that fleshly sin gets defeated, producing what verse 11 calls the "harvest of righteousness."

Embrace Your Complete Forgiveness

Here is the bottom line: Do you believe God has completely forgiven you for your past, present, and future sins? I'm not asking if you feel like God has forgiven you. You may not. In fact, you may have been carrying around a lot of unnecessary guilt for a long time. It's time to let that guilt go by faith. Not based on how you feel, but on the fact of your complete forgiveness.

Take a moment right now to accept God's complete forgiveness. Feel free to use the following prayer as a starting point:

Father, based on your Word, I believe Jesus Christ died on the cross to pay for all my sins. I believe because of this, I am forgiven in Christ for all the sins in my past, my present, and my future. I also believe the punishment for my sins was placed on him and that you will never be angry with me or punish me. When I sin in the future, remind me to run toward you, not away from you. Then I can tell you my sin with the confidence that I am already forgiven. Remind me that I can repent, not promising to do better next time but turning to Jesus Christ in me. Then I can ask him to live through me so I don't do it again but obey my Father instead. Thank you for loving me so much that I am completely forgiven now and forever. Amen.

8

Christians Are Designed to Become Stronger in Suffering

Would you be surprised if I told you Christianity is easier than you think because of suffering? That may sound contradictory, but it's true. Our loving Father often reveals to us the life-giving power of his best-kept secret in the New Covenant through our personal suffering.

Earlier I told you about when the church I had founded was failing. It was a real time of crisis for me, and therefore my family. Over the next few years my situation got so bad it seemed as though my life was falling apart. I was doing my best to obey and serve God, but he was allowing one difficulty after another.

I was unable to love my sweet wife, Ellen, like I wanted to. Don't misunderstand; we didn't have a terrible relationship. And she was not my problem. My problem was an inability within me to feel and express genuine love for her. I felt totally frustrated about this struggle, but I was incapable of changing it.

At the same time, my closest friends pulled away from me for no apparent reason. It wasn't that we had conflicts. Each of them just seemed to be too busy and somewhat disconnected from our relationship. I felt isolated and rejected.

My struggles eventually moved from my mind into my body. I began to experience pain in my upper and lower back, which added another layer to my angst and discouragement.

In the midst of it all, a scene crept into my mind one day as I gazed at our small kitchen table. For some reason I envisioned each leg falling off, one by one, until the tabletop fell flat on the floor. This felt like what was happening in my life. Just like each of the legs, everything I had relied on to give me meaning in life had fallen off, one by one. Like that tabletop, I now had no one and no circumstances to prop me up. I felt more alone than I ever had in my life. I sunk into a dungeon of emotional darkness, where depression and anxiety constantly lurked.

Worst of all, God seemed completely silent.

Finally, all this suffering brought me to the end of my rope. Then as my strength gave out, I had to let go of it. I just couldn't go on living this kind of Christianity. I was done. I did not have the mental, emotional, or physical strength to do it.

My heavenly dad then spoke the life-giving words of grace I didn't even know I needed to hear. "Mark, even if this church fails, I still accept you."

Starting the next day, I became so full of God's love that it changed me forever. Now I could express deep love for Ellen. My depression was replaced with joy. My physical pains began to subside. And it no longer mattered that my friends were absent from my life, because Jesus was my best friend.

God had a specific plan he had been carrying out through my suffering, but I had been blind to it. God had been loving me by letting my life fall apart, using all my losses and struggles to bring me to this point.

Why? For the most important purpose he has for every Christian. He wanted to reveal Jesus Christ in me as my all in all. He wanted to glorify himself through this revelation of his Son in me. He wanted me to finally understand that Jesus Christ alone is my life, as Colossians 3:4 says: "When Christ, who is our life, is revealed, then you also will be revealed with Him in glory" (NASB). He wanted to reveal to me that Christ being my life is abundant life as well as eternal life because he *is* all of that! Once he did, the sun came out, brightly warming my soul with his great love for me, and the thick fog of gloom burned away.

My suffering had a surprise ending that I wouldn't have imagined while I was going through it. That's often the secret about suffering for Christians we counsel and teach. The surprise ending is the revelation of Jesus Christ in us that frees and heals us in ways nothing or no one else can.

This doesn't mean we will never struggle or suffer again. But it does mean Christianity will be easier than we ever thought. Why? Because we will be living more and more from a place of relying on Jesus Christ in us. That's what it means when I say God designed us as Christians to become stronger in suffering—through his strength, not ours.

As you can see from my life, our desperation is often God's preparation for his revelation!

Christianity Is Not an Escape from Suffering

It doesn't matter if you are a Christian or not, you are going to experience suffering in this world. In fact, we are told we will definitely experience suffering. Jesus famously said, "Here on earth you will have many trials and sorrows" (John 16:33 NLT).

Peter wrote this about suffering: "Dear friends, don't be surprised at the fiery trials you are going through, as if something strange were happening to you" (1 Peter 4:12 NLT).

What is suffering? In general, we can say suffering is personal pain caused by life issues.

A big question we all want the answer to is, "What causes us to suffer?" The ultimate reason suffering comes upon us is because Adam and Eve sinned. We now all live in a messed-up world with messed-up people and messed-up bodies.

Causes more specific, however, also exist.

- Suffering *others bring on us*, such as rejection, divorce, betrayal, abuse—or persecution, like for some of my friends in Pakistan.
- Suffering *we bring on ourselves* from the sins we commit, such as worrying, unforgiveness, or adultery. This suffering also includes mistakes like bad financial decisions or not seeing the other car before we pull in front of it.
- Suffering that's a result of *circumstances beyond our control.* This includes events or circumstances like job loss through no fault of our own, a child born with a mental or physical disability, unexplained health problems, or the loss of people precious to us.
- Suffering caused by *our ignorance of the New Covenant,* which results in natural consequences from living according to the flesh instead of walking in the Spirit. This includes feelings of condemnation, frustration, and defeat.
- Suffering caused by *the spiritual attacks Satan inflicts on our lives.* This includes lies he tempts us to believe about God, ourselves, other people, and life events.

Can God remove our suffering? Yes, he can, but it seems as though most of the time he doesn't. The great news, though, is that God is bigger than our suffering. He can use it for his purposes to bring himself glory through his sufficient grace.

Paul believed God could remove his own personal suffering, which is why he asked him to do so. We can pray that too. But God had a different purpose for Paul, just as he often does for each of us as his sons and daughters in Christ. He explains this precisely in 2 Corinthians 12:8–9: "Three different times I begged the Lord to take it away. Each time he said, 'My grace is all you need. My power works best in weakness.' So now I am glad to boast about my weaknesses, so that the power of Christ can work through me" (NLT).

Don't Quote Romans 8:28 When Someone Is Suffering

I have felt like punching another Christian only a few times. Most of those times came when I had just finished sharing about a time of suffering I or one of my family members had been experiencing.

And then they shared a Bible verse with me. You've probably heard this one too. "And we know that in all things God works for the good of those who love him, who have been called according to his purpose" (Rom. 8:28).

I felt like punching them because, instead of responding with God's compassion, they seemed to be trying to "fix" me with this Scripture. I needed to be reminded of the truth in Romans 8:28 later, not in a time of great pain. Ill-timed truth can be hurtful, not helpful.

Nonetheless, it's a great verse that assures us God can take the good and the bad in our lives and cause them to work together for good. This "good" is first and foremost to conform us to the image of Christ, according to the next verse, Romans 8:29: "For those God foreknew he also predestined to be conformed to the image of his Son, that he might be the firstborn among many brothers and sisters."

This brings about a deeper intimacy with God for us and gives greater expression of him through us to bless other people. Other times, it can include blessings in our lives we can clearly see. For example, a few years ago my oldest son, Andrew, kept calling my phone while Ellen and I were at a movie with our daughter Bekah.

When I finally got up and called him, he said, "Dad, it's okay now, but I caught the house on fire."

"What happened?" I said, alarmed.

"I was upstairs watching TV. In a little while, Christopher yelled out to me, 'Andrew, why is there smoke coming up the stairs?' I had placed a pan of cooking oil on the stove to get hot so I could fry some shrimp. But when I went upstairs, I forgot about it. I freaked out when I saw that the pan and the cabinets above it were on fire. Christopher wanted to throw water on it, but I told him we'd better use the fire extinguisher. We put the fire out, but there's still smoke everywhere."

When we got home, we saw the stove and microwave above it had melted. The cabinets were charred. The ceiling and walls downstairs had black soot everywhere. We were all stunned, but mainly glad Andrew and Christopher were safe.

Now for the good: Ellen had been wanting to change the color of the paint on our walls. She got her wish. Our homeowners insurance paid for new paint, which was the exact color she wanted. We also got a new stove, a new microwave, and newly painted cabinets. Romans 8:28, right? We saw the "good" very obviously.

Sometimes, however, Romans 8:28 and even verse 29 are not so obvious. For example, my twenty-five-year-old daughter, Bekah, was born with Down syndrome. Due largely to Ellen's relentless work with her from the day of her birth, Bekah overcame all odds by eventually becoming a full-time student at the University of South Carolina in a special program. When she arrived, she was an outgoing, fun-loving young woman who absolutely loved college. It was the highlight of her life.

Suddenly, with only one semester left in her four-year program, she descended into a confused, pitiful shell of the person she had been. It erased most of the joyful, outgoing, dancing person we knew.

Why? Over two years ago, she developed a severe headache. This landed her in the emergency room, where our world blew up in a matter of minutes. While waiting for the doctor, Bekah had a complete psychotic breakdown. She fell to the floor, screaming as loud as she could, "Don't hit me. Don't hit me!" Ellen and I were horrified, wondering what in the world was causing her to hallucinate.

Bekah was quickly admitted to the hospital, where they performed every imaginable test to diagnose what was wrong. While there, she would tell us someone was under her bed. She tried to get up every few minutes to look under the bed, no matter how many times we attempted to convince her no one was there.

She also had other irrational fears. Because of this, she would sit on the floor behind her hospital room door, determined to stay there all night. She was in such a state of anxiety, the doctors had to give her megadoses of pain, anxiety, and sleep medications. This combination and doses of medicines would have knocked out two giant football players, but it didn't work for Bekah. She sat there night after night. My wife and I felt very afraid of what we were seeing.

When he could find no organic reason for Bekah's behavior, her psychiatrist chocked it up to months of sleep deprivation due to a traumatic event. He sent her home with psychiatric medication.

Over the next three months, Bekah saw fourteen different doctors, but we got no closer to a diagnosis than in the beginning. Yet her vitality and health were continuing to deteriorate. She was losing weight, becoming listless, and could no longer feed herself.

In desperation, we got Bekah an appointment with a neurologist at Duke University Medical Center, but we'd have to wait ten days to see him. During that time, she deteriorated so greatly that Ellen and I prayed she wouldn't die before her appointment. It was absolutely terrifying.

At her appointment, the doctor told us he suspected an autoimmune disease was attacking her brain. He immediately admitted her to the hospital, telling us he was going to give her 1,000 mg of steroids intravenously every day. If she improved at all, it would confirm his diagnosis. He proved to be correct.

Now, however, even after many other treatments with immunosuppressant drugs, Bekah is only 20 percent the person she used to be. She continues to be treated and has been prayed for by many people, but her brain has been so affected that this young woman who was once vibrant, loving, outgoing, and loved by everyone now sits on our couch all day, speaks nonsensical phrases, and sometimes screams at the top of her lungs when it's time to go to bed.

As I write this book, we still do not know the end of this story. What we do know is that it has turned our entire family's life upside down. We remain exhausted and emotionally vulnerable. Our hearts still feel sad many days, wondering where this is all going.

Though we trust God in all this, we don't see Romans 8:28 for Bekah or our family. To be honest, I have to admit we haven't appreciated people quoting this verse to us. It's not what we have needed to hear. We've found the most help from people who have just loved us through it. That is what everyone needs when they are experiencing suffering, not someone quoting Romans 8:28.

Yet I want you to know we believe the message in Romans 8:28–29 is true. Whether people quote these verses to us inappropriately or whether we see it played out in this circumstance, it's still true. It's possible that we will never see what this trial means this side of heaven, but I will say again that the message is true.

I will add this. These words in this book were written in the fiery crucible of this suffering. While numerous concerns, fears, and stresses have swirled around me and definitely affected me, when I have written, there has been a tangible sense of a deep joy and intimacy with God. He's still somehow involved in all of it.

God Is Not Trying to Build Character in You through Suffering

Sometimes we need to attack the incorrect sacred cows in our Christian belief system. For instance, when many Christians experience suffering, they believe God is trying to build character in them. This idea is a misconception. I'll even go so far as to say it's one of the biggest misconceptions among Christians.

I've heard several people say with a resigned sigh, "I sure wish God would stop trying to build character in me! I've had enough suffering for a while!"

The truth is God is not trying to build character *in* you when you suffer. It's the opposite. He's trying to get character *out of* you, because it's already there! You have all the character you will ever need already in you. In fact, you've had it in you from the moment you believed in Jesus Christ for your salvation. Colossians 2:10 says, "In Him you have been made complete" (NASB).

To be complete in Christ means you have all the character of Christ already in you! This is in your spirit, which is your identity in Christ. This is Jesus Christ in you. God uses our life challenges, however, as opportunities to trust Christ in us so that this character can come out. As we spiritually mature, the character of his life in our spirit becomes more and more consistently displayed in our souls and through our lives. This clarifies the truth that our spirits are perfectly saved. Our souls are being saved and our bodies will be saved.

That is what proven character means in Romans 5:3–4: "We also exult in our tribulations, knowing that tribulation brings about perseverance; and perseverance, proven character; and proven character, hope" (NASB).

During my years as a legalist, a religious Christian, I was convinced God wanted to build character in me. I saw God as primarily a teacher who used all of life to teach me how he wanted to build character in my life.

It was exciting at first, and I wanted to cooperate with God in this. I even had cards with certain character traits written on them with definitions. For example, for the character trait of patience, I defined it as the ability to stay calm instead of getting angry when life didn't go my way. So when I ended up at the emergency room because my three-year-old was bitten by my parents' dog, I tried to be patient. I felt some anger, but I shoved it down and acted calm.

Do you see what I did? I "tried" to be patient. I shoved my anger down and "acted" calm. Do you know what that was? It was my religious flesh trying to be patient. It wasn't genuine patience. No wonder my anger would come out on Ellen at times.

After a long time of working on patience and many other character traits, like kindness and humility, I took my cards to Ellen and asked her, "Do you see any of these character traits in me?" She read each of them, and as gently as she knew how, she told me I was doing "okay." It was her nice way of saying, "Maybe a little, but not much."

After a few more months of trying to help God build character in my life, I finally got tired of trying so hard and threw the cards in the back of a desk drawer.

Within the next year I had come to the end of my spiritual rope, as I shared earlier. Remember, that was when I began to trust Christ to live his life through me. Shortly after this, I was looking for something in my desk and came upon those character trait cards. I grabbed them and found Ellen. "Do you see any of these character traits in me now?"

When she read them, she said, "I see all of them in you." What had made the difference in her response this time? As a result of God's work through my suffering, she had been seeing Jesus Christ live and love through me.

Jesus has all those character traits. He is patience, kindness, love, and so much more. You see, with him in me I had all the "proven character" I needed. He was simply working to get it out of me, so to speak.

This proven character is what God wants to bring forth from you when you go through suffering. For example, I mentioned I had worked on patience. That's a trait many people commonly pray God will give them.

But did you know you never need to ask God for patience? You have all the patience you will ever need already in you because you have Christ in you. It's also who you are in Christ. You are a patient person in Christ.

When I'm sitting in traffic and realize I'm going to be late or I'm tired and want to get home, I can feel frustration and impatience desiring to control me. When that happens, I say out loud, "Jesus, in you I already have all the patience I need for this situation. In fact, because of my identity in Christ, I am a patient person." Usually as soon as I speak this truth to myself, I experience peace.

As Christians, we also have all the love we will ever need. We have all the joy and peace we will ever need. This doesn't mean we feel love, joy, and peace all the time. It also doesn't mean we remember what we have all the time. We don't. But it's still true.

Part of God's best-kept secret is that we already have all the character and strength we will ever need within us through Christ when we suffer. Only when we accept this truth can we understand what it means to rely on Christ in us and to truly believe in who we are in him.

Satan Lies to You When You Suffer

When we experience suffering, Satan often whispers negative thoughts to us. Though his intelligence is thousands of times greater than ours, he is fairly predictable. During our suffering, he puts negative thoughts in our minds about God, ourselves, other people, circumstances, and the future. For example, when you've experienced difficulty, have you ever had any of the following thoughts?

- God must be angry with me about something I've done wrong.
- If I were a better Christian, I would be able to handle life's difficulties better.
- If my wife [or husband] would change, I would be happy in life.
- Life is about becoming a stronger person in every situation. I need to improve.

Satan's goal is to destroy us any way he can. Remember, John 10:10 tells us, "The thief comes only to steal and kill and destroy" (NASB). One of his first goals is to discourage us to the point that we take our focus off Jesus and put it on our circumstances.

Here is a good example of this. John sat down and said to me, "I'm here for counseling because, ever since my dad died, I've been very depressed. I know depression is a normal part of the grieving process, but I've been stuck for six months."

Over the next few weeks, John told me how close he had been to his father and asked me questions. As I probed more about what thoughts he was having, I began to realize Satan was whispering some specific things into John's mind. I believed they were the source of why he was stuck. Let me share the answers I gave to his questions from the second half of Romans 8. This New Covenant Scripture is all about suffering and how we can overcome through Jesus Christ and his love in that suffering.

I helped him realize each of his questions, essentially common among Christians, was based on Satan's lies.

John's first question was, "Do you think God is disappointed with me, since I just can't pray right now?" The answer is in Romans 8:26: "In the same way the Spirit also helps our weakness; for we do not know how to pray as we should, but the Spirit

Himself intercedes for us with groanings too deep for words" (NASB).

When you are in deep suffering, you often want to pray but can't. The words just will not come. When this happens, you need to be assured there is no condemnation from God. The Holy Spirit is praying for you even when you can't pray. In other words, he is praying perfect prayers for you to your Father, who is going to answer them in a perfect way. So don't worry. God is not disappointed. He's got you covered.

John's second question was, "Is God punishing me for a sin I committed by taking my dad away from me?" God anticipated that Satan would put this accusing lie in our minds during our suffering. He gives a clear answer to help us overcome this lie in Romans 8:33–34: "Who will bring a charge against God's elect? God is the one who justifies; who is the one who condemns? Christ Jesus is He who died, yes, rather who was raised, who is at the right hand of God, who also intercedes for us" (NASB).

God's answer is that he is not punishing you and is never going to punish you. He has removed any punishment for your sins by justifying you. Remember, being justified means we are as righteous as Jesus. God has no need to punish you for a sin because he punished Jesus on our behalf instead and then made you righteous. Based on that, Jesus is praying for you too.

The third question John asked me was, "If God really loves me, why did he let my dad die? And why is he letting me go through this depression?" Satan puts the thought in many Christians' minds that their suffering proves God doesn't love them, because if he did he wouldn't be allowing it.

Let's let God speak to us in Romans 8:38–39. "For I am convinced that neither death, nor life, nor angels, nor principalities, nor things present, nor things to come, nor powers, nor height, nor depth, nor any other created thing, will be able to separate us from the love of God, which is in Christ Jesus our Lord" (NASB).

God gives you the truth you need to defeat Satan's lies by making sure you are confident that nothing can separate you from his love. He is telling us nothing we will ever experience will be able to separate us from his love for us. To make sure we know our suffering is not proof that he does not love us, he makes a big point of telling us where his love is. Do you see it at the very end of verse 39? "In Christ Jesus our Lord."

Where are you right now? You are "in Christ." Where is God's love for you found? In Christ. You can never be separated from God's love for you. He's affirming to you that in your suffering he still loves you.

Once John understood God's answers to his questions, we spent the next few weeks going over one more truth—that God's purpose in his suffering was to conform him to the image of Christ, according to Romans 8:29: "For those God foreknew he also predestined to be conformed to the image of his Son, that he might be the firstborn among many brothers and sisters." To be conformed to the image of Jesus means to live more and more like who Christ is in us.

It wasn't long before John's depression was replaced with a deep peace rooted in his confidence that God's love for him was real and proven. Because of John's suffering, his relationship with God was enhanced. Satan was defeated and Jesus was exalted!

Suffering Can Bring Spiritual Brokenness

True "spiritual brokenness" is a positive term. It speaks of a process God often takes his children through for a specific purpose. It's not the kind of brokenness of prisoners who have lost all hope. It's more like the brokenness of the self-will of a child whom a parent loves. As a loving parent, God must often break our dependence on the flesh—not because he is angry with us, but because he loves us and has something better for us. Suffering is most often the main ingredient in this process he uses to accomplish true spiritual brokenness.

The word *brokenness* is used to describe many issues people struggle with today. I want to be sensitive to those struggles, but I also want to clarify what I am not talking about when I speak of brokenness. Some people need healing and freedom from many kinds of brokenness.

With that in mind, let me acknowledge other ways the word *brokenness* is used. "Emotional brokenness" is often used to describe people in deep emotional pain because of what has happened to them, but they are not yet healed. "Sexual brokenness" is often used to describe people who have been sexually abused and are not yet healed. We are all "broken," a general term used to describe how, in many ways, we are all messed up because we live in a sinful world. These are all valid uses of the word *brokenness*, but they are not spiritual brokenness.

Let me say it again. Spiritual brokenness is not a negative term but a positive one. It speaks of a loving process our Father wants to bring us through so we can experience the Christian life as he intended it. Because God is sovereign, he uses the hard times of our lives to bring about spiritual brokenness.

In our ministry, we teach people that spiritual brokenness is a threefold process.

1. Brokenness reveals our flesh and its bankruptcy.
2. Brokenness frees us from our consistent reliance on our flesh.
3. Brokenness reveals Christ in us so that we rely on him instead.

Ephesians 3:16–17 points to why all Christians need this when it says, "I pray that out of his glorious riches he may strengthen you with power through his Spirit in your inner being, so that Christ may dwell in your hearts through faith."

The majority of Christians know the *fact* that Jesus Christ dwells in them. Yet they may still be living dependent on the flesh. What this prayer tells us is that not every Christian knows how to live by *faith* in Christ in them. That is what brokenness brings about—a revelation of Christ in us so we can live by faith in him daily as we never have before.

God often brings spiritual brokenness about when we experience failure, defeat, emotional pain, and our inability to fix ourselves or our relationships. I meet a lot of people, however, who say they have been broken, when what they are really saying is they have experienced suffering. Brokenness and suffering are not the same.

A Christian can suffer and be broken in some of the other ways I mentioned. But that does not automatically mean they are spiritually broken.

In 2 Corinthians 4:11–12, Paul describes his own spiritual brokenness: "We who are alive are always being given over to death for Jesus' sake, so that his life may also be revealed in our mortal body. So then, death is at work in us, but life is at work in you."

Paul had once been a prideful religious leader. After he met Jesus, time and time again he was humbled through his suffering. This humbling did not occur to make Paul miserable. This Scripture says it occurred so that the life of Jesus would be revealed in Paul. Its end result glorified God as Jesus lived through Paul in a broader and more powerful ministry to others.

You may wonder, *Does my life have to fall apart to experience spiritual brokenness?* Not necessarily. God knows what each of us needs for this to happen. Is it a one-time process? No, although there seems to be an initial spiritual brokenness in Christians that gets us started. Then it may be repeated many times in our lives as what might be termed "miniature" versions of it.

When does it occur in our spiritual journey? For some it's at the moment of salvation. For others it's a result of burnout after a time of lengthy service for God. For still others it's after personal or relational problems nothing seems to help.

One of my friends, Mike, experienced spiritual brokenness. He was a wonderful pastor. Everyone loved him, and he had all the outward appearances of a successful ministry.

But when Mike came to see me, he said, "Very few people know my marriage is a mess. That's because what people see is that God has blessed me with a very successful ministry. What they don't see is the many days of hurtful arguing and yelling at home. It seems as though there is never any resolution. My wife and I live with little emotional closeness and we both feel miserable in our marriage. She tells me the only reason I stay in the marriage is because I don't want to destroy my reputation. I tell her the only reason she stays with me is because I make all the money.

"I've read lots of Christian books in an attempt to fix my marriage, but she doesn't do anything. All she does is complain and tell me everything I do is wrong. If I'm being honest, I have to admit I've been trying to fix my wife for years. But I can't fix her and I can't fix my marriage. I don't want a divorce, but I don't know what to do. That's why I'm here."

Mike and his wife were both suffering in a loveless marriage because they were living according to their flesh. The flesh can never produce genuine love. After we spent many hours in New Covenant–based counseling, Mike was ready for God to work in his own life. On that day I asked him some questions, and Mike's answers showed me God had prepared him for this moment in counseling.

"Mike, do you believe God has shown you that you have an issue with pride?"

"Yes, he has convinced me of that in our time of counseling. I have acted prideful in my ministry and in my marriage. I've had the attitude that I am God's amazing gift to the church and to my wife. It makes me sick to think of it, but it's true."

"Do you also realize that in many ways your wife is correct about why you are staying with her? I believe God wants your marriage to work, but are you staying with her because of your reputation as a pastor? Is it possible that you have built your personal sense of identity from your ministry instead of resting in your identity in Christ, as we have been seeing in Scripture?"

Mike hung his head and admitted that was all true.

"And do you understand that all of this ultimately means you have been relying on your flesh instead of Christ in you?"

"Yes, I do, and I'm ready to give that up."

"Let's talk about giving up our rights for a minute."

We read in Philippians 2:5–11 that Jesus gave up his rights:

> You must have the same attitude that Christ Jesus had. Though he was God, he did not think of equality with God as something to cling to. Instead, he gave up his divine privileges; he took the humble position of a slave and was born as a human being. When he appeared in human form, he humbled himself in obedience to God and died a criminal's death on a cross. Therefore, God elevated him to the place of highest honor and gave him the name above all other names, that at the name of Jesus every knee should bow, in heaven and on earth and under the earth, and every tongue declare that Jesus Christ is Lord, to the glory of God the Father. (NLT)

Then I said, "Jesus gave up his legitimate rights to hold on to his equality with God. Instead, he was willing to become a slave as a human being. He was also willing to humble himself and obey God and die a criminal's death. As a result God exalted him as the Lord of everything and everybody for God the Father's glory.

"Mike, God often asks us to give up our rights too. Some of your rights are legitimate, like your right for your wife to live faithful to you. She, too, has that same legitimate right, for you to live faithful to her. Some of our rights, though, are not legitimate.

"For example, it's fine to desire your wife's love and respect, but you can't demand it. If you are demanding it, you've turned your desire into an expectation, which puts your wife under your law. In other words, you have put her under a standard you expect her to live up to for you. God doesn't want us to put people under law, but under grace. Once we have put them under our own law, we are living with an illegitimate right.

"Do you understand how you have been requiring your wife to live under your own imposed laws for her? Do you understand that you have been holding on to rights?"

"Yes, I sure do," Mike said.

"Whether a right is legitimate or illegitimate, God often wants us to give them up to him. These rights can be our flesh's attempts to be in control so we can try to meet our needs for security, competence, acceptance, love, and esteem from a source other than God. Giving up our rights may be what God uses to bring about the spiritual brokenness we have been talking about. It's a matter of being willing to give up these rights, if that is what is needed to have a revelation of Christ in us as our all in all. In your case, if God could use you giving up your rights for this reason, would you be willing to do that?

"For example, what if you gave God the right for your wife to love and respect you the way you think she should? What if you gave God the right to have a happy marriage the way you think it should be? Do you see where I'm going with this?"

"Yes, and I am willing to give up these rights and any others God shows me," Mike said. "I want to know Jesus in me more than I want my wife's love and even more than I want my reputation as a great pastor at the church."

I could see the Holy Spirit was working in Mike to show him even more rights he may need to give up to God. I suggested that he may need to give up the right to

good circumstances
good health
avoid suffering

friendships
a happy marriage
obedient children
be married
his reputation
a successful ministry or job
possessions
money
good feelings

Then I said, "Mike, are you ready to humble yourself before God by telling him you're sorry about your sin of pride? Are you willing to give up the rights God wants you to give up? Are you willing to admit to him that you have built your identity in your reputation as a pastor instead of in Christ? And finally, do you want to ask God to do whatever it takes to reveal Jesus Christ in you as your perfect source for life?"

Mike didn't hesitate. "I'm willing to do all that if that is what God wants to use to reveal Christ in me," he said. "I want that more than anything in this world."

Mike had tears streaming down his face. Then he prayed a prayer I will invite you to also pray in just a moment. It wasn't immediate, but several weeks later God answered Mike's prayer. He revealed to Mike that not his ministry, his reputation, or his marriage was his source for life. Christ in him was his only perfect source of life.

Mike experienced great freedom and emotional healing as he was broken of his default way of living dependent on the flesh. His anger with his wife was replaced with a deep, genuine love for her that came from Christ in him. He was a happier man in his home, and his wife noticed. At first, she was skeptical. But over time she began to realize the change was real. He experienced a new default way to live by faith on Christ in him.

Unfortunately, she was not willing to stop relying on her flesh. She didn't change and remained miserable in her own pain. But Mike was free. He spoke the truth to her when necessary, but he no longer tried to fix her or the marriage. To this day, Mike continues to trust Christ in him to love his wife as much as she will let him. He also enjoys his ministry even more now that Christ is the source of his identity.

How to Gauge Your Growth through Brokenness

How do you know if you've experienced spiritual brokenness? Here are some clues I've seen among the hundreds of Christians I've counseled. I'm not implying perfect behavior or attitudes, but rather a shift in mind-set. When the following changes occur, we tend to be moving our focus to a deeper dependency upon Christ.

- You begin to believe God's love for you in a much deeper way.
- Your emotional pain begins to be healed.
- Family and friends begin to feel more accepted by you. (Not sure? Just ask them.)
- Your default mode throughout the day moves to relying on Jesus to live through you in your job, relationships, health, hobbies, ministry work—everything.
- When concerns arise, you learn to take them to God and let him handle your stress.
- You experience more victory over harmful habits you couldn't conquer before.
- You accept yourself and appreciate the way God made your personality and body.
- You recognize your self-reliant, fleshly strategies more often, but realize they don't define you. Your identity in Christ defines you.

- You desire to obey God out of love for him, not out of forced obligation.
- A growing sense of confidence centers on who you are in Christ, not your behavior, failures, successes, clothes, ministry, family, or the opinions of others.

From God's perspective, it's necessary for every Christian to experience spiritual brokenness. You and I can expect trials and tough times on this fallen planet. Since this is true, how can you cooperate with God when suffering occurs? Keep these four important New Covenant points in mind:

1. Become familiar with the truth of God's unconditional love and acceptance, and the power he offers to live within you, as described throughout Scripture and this book.
2. Realize that your fleshly strategies of self-dependence are the ultimate problem that prevents you from experiencing Christ in you.
3. Openly tell God you believe his truth, whether or not you feel it. Ask him to reprogram your mind by reinforcing the revelation of Christ in you.
4. Don't be concerned with how quickly your circumstances will change or how fast you grow in your Christian walk. Don't focus on yourself; focus on Jesus.

Would you like to pray to accept that your own spiritual brokenness is God's plan for you personally? Remember, he plans for you to be spiritually broken because he wants what is best for you. It's not because he is angry. He's a loving Father. With that in mind, as you process your own suffering and growth, consider the encouragement found in the following prayer:

Dear Father, I realize I need spiritual brokenness in my own life and only you can bring this about for me. I understand that my flesh is preventing me from experiencing Christ living in and through me the way you designed me to live. I give up these rights to you. [Use the list of possible rights earlier in this chapter and add others God may show you to help you here.] *I give you permission to use whatever is necessary to reveal the bankruptcy of the flesh to me, to free me from my consistent reliance on the flesh, and to reveal Christ in me so I can rely on him more and more. I pray this in Jesus's name, Amen.*

Spiritual brokenness through our suffering is greatly needed for us to experience deeper intimacy with God. May you open your eyes to this marvelous New Covenant truth so that it remains part of the secret no longer!

9

Christians Will Not Feel Free unless They Forgive

Many people may believe forgiving is an important issue but never realize the essential part it plays in our lives.

Michael and Isabella came to me for marriage counseling. After our initial introduction, Michael blurted, "Our pastor sent us to you to help put our marriage back together. But we don't know if we are going to make it." His face began to tighten with an angry look, so I asked, "What makes you say that?"

"Recently, I caught Isabella committing adultery. She was supposed to have been on a fun trip with some friends. But when I saw one of those friends at church, I got suspicious. I drove three hours to the hotel in another town where I thought she was. The hotel door was unlocked, and I walked inside and found her in bed with another man! I'm so incredibly hurt and angry that I can hardly stand it. I don't *want* to divorce Isabella. We're both

Christians and we have two kids together. But I just can't forgive her for what she did to me and our family."

Obviously, this was a serious crisis, and Michael and Isabella faced a difficult situation. It's easy to think Isabella's betrayal could never make her worthy of forgiveness. I told them, "I believe if you'll hang in there with me, God can bring a deep healing to your marriage. But the one thing I ask is that you stay in counseling, especially when we discuss the issue of forgiveness. Are you willing to do that?" They both nodded in agreement.

After twenty years of counseling, I've discovered one of the most misunderstood concepts in Christianity is how to forgive God's way. Forgiving God's way is an intentional choice to release someone who has offended us from what we believe they owe us, such as love, respect, or acceptance. The power of true forgiveness can then unleash a level of freedom and healing like nothing else.

Many Christians Misunderstand True Forgiveness

I've never met a person who didn't need to forgive someone. Never. The sad reality is that many Christians know they need to forgive, but they harbor the resentment. Some think they have forgiven, but the process was left unfinished. Their lack of forgiveness becomes a heavy, silent burden they carry for years, which they may not even be aware of.

We can erroneously think we have forgiven someone for any number of reasons. We don't think about what happened anymore. We pray for the other person. We act nice to the other person. We ask the other person to forgive us. We ask God to forgive the other person. None of these actions, however, represents true forgiveness. What is true forgiveness? Let's start with Jesus's words to his disciple, Peter. In Matthew 18:21–35, Peter asks, "Lord, how often shall my brother sin against me and I forgive him? Up to seven times?" (NASB).

The religious leaders and rabbis of that time taught that a person needed to forgive someone only three times, so Peter was more than doubling the current standard. He was asking Jesus if forgiving someone seven times is enough.

Jesus told Peter to forgive seven times seventy, which is 490 times. This number was so high that what he meant was, "Peter, you always forgive."

It makes you wonder who this person was who was offending Peter over and over. Was it his wife? Was it his kid? Was it one of the other disciples of Jesus?

Let's face it. Sometimes it's difficult to forgive someone for even one offense they've committed against us. Yet Jesus is telling you and me the same thing he told Peter. We are to always forgive. Why? God has forgiven us completely. We are like our heavenly Father in that we are forgivers in our identity in Christ.

This does not mean God wants you to be hurt over and over again without confronting it. (See Matt. 18:15–16.) But regardless of the steps you may take to protect yourself, you still need to forgive.

As he often did, Jesus tells a story to teach about forgiveness. In this story in Matthew 18:23–35, the king represents God, the first slave represents you, and the second slave represents people you need to forgive.

The king discovers the first slave owes him about ten million dollars in today's money. This represents the debt we each owe God. This debt is for the many, many sins God holds us responsible for that we will commit from the day we are born until the day we die.

The slave deserved to be punished for not being able to repay the debt he owed the king, just like we deserve to be punished by God for every sin we commit. This man begged for mercy, and the king gave it to him though he did not deserve it. In the same way, God had mercy on us in Christ and forgave us when we did not deserve it.

We would think that this slave, forgiven of his debt, would be happy to forgive the comparatively small debt another slave owed him. Instead he threw him into prison. In the same way, because God has forgiven us for our many sins, it would seem to make sense, then, that we would forgive people who owe us honesty, love, respect, protection, and so on. Yet we still struggle to forgive them. Why?

We put people in the prison of our minds and keep mulling over what they did and what we wish we could say or do to them to let them "have it." We want them to hurt like we hurt. Doing this, though, keeps us in prison, too, because bitterness and resentment hurts us, not them!

Have you heard the saying "Hurt people hurt people"? How true that is! When you harbor unforgiveness toward someone, it not only hurts you; it hurts the people you care about. You may lash out at your spouse, children, or friends because you have not forgiven them or someone else. On the flip side, "Healed people heal people." That's another reason forgiving people is so important.

If you have really deep wounds, you may need help facing your pain so you can forgive. Yet Jesus still wants you to forgive. He knows it will give you great healing and freedom.

Reasons for Not Forgiving Are Never Justified

People often come up with reasons they think justify not forgiving someone. Some of the most common justifications include,

1. *We are waiting for them to admit they offended us.* If we wait for that, we may wait forever, because they may not even know or believe they did anything wrong.

2. *We believe they don't deserve to be forgiven because of how badly they hurt us.* You are right, except you didn't deserve for God to forgive you either, but he did anyway.

3. *We want to punish them for what they did to us.* The only person being punished when we don't forgive is us. Offending parties are going on with their lives and may not even

be thinking about what happened, while we are living in emotional pain every day.

4. *We don't want to stir up hurtful feelings by thinking about what they did to us.* We're fearful it will make us feel out of control. That's understandable to a point, but the fear of facing what happened can prevent our healing. That is why we sometimes need a trusted pastor or New Covenant counselor to help us.

5. *We think if we forgive we are saying what they did was okay.* Actually, it's the opposite. Forgiving someone is acknowledging that what that person did was wrong.

6. *We believe as long as we stay angry with them we won't be hurt by them again.* But unresolved anger may do the opposite, making us overly sensitive to legitimate or perceived hurts by them.

7. *We believe we have to tell them we forgive them.* The truth is you only need to forgive people before God. The only exception to that is if people come to you first and ask for forgiveness specifically for what they did to offend you.

8. *We are afraid that if we forgive them, it means we can keep letting them hurt us.* That may or may not be true. Sometimes God wants us to let it go and pray for the people who hurt us to come to an understanding of what they are doing. But most of the time we need to confront them. We definitely should not allow abuse by someone. If you are in that situation, please reach out for help from your pastor or a New Covenant counselor. You may also need to call the national or local abuse hotline.

9. *We confuse reconciliation with forgiveness.* Reconciliation means after we forgive people we reenter relationships with them. That's the ideal, but it may not always be possible. We always need to forgive, but we may not always be able to reconcile, such as in the case of sexual abuse.

Forgiving Doesn't Mean Forgetting

When my daughter, Bekah, was in middle school, she asked us if she could participate in cheerleader tryouts. Even though she has Down syndrome, we encouraged her, and she began to attend the afterschool practices.

My wife and I were amazed when Bekah came home and did cheers for us, shouting the words correctly along with doing splits, jumps, and hand claps. We thought if she made the team, it would be great physical activity for her, and great for the school to have a teen with disabilities representing them at games. We also saw it as a way to help teens overcome prejudices against people with disabilities.

On the final day of tryouts, each girl performed a cheer and the cheerleading coach decided who made the cut. Unfortunately, Bekah did not make the team. Like other girls who didn't make it, she was really disappointed.

But then we got a shock. We received an anonymous letter from someone claiming to be a parent. It basically stated that Bekah didn't belong with "normal" girls on the team and she should have never tried out in the first place. We were stunned. We were greatly puzzled by this letter, but soon we began to stew inside with frustration and deep anger toward this anonymous parent. As you can imagine, Ellen and I felt offended because we had seen this type of prejudice before, and now my precious daughter had been maligned by this parent.

We found ourselves facing a big choice. We could forgive, or we could live in the deception that Christians often face—thinking by holding on to our anger and stewing inside, it would somehow hurt the other person. But that would have hurt us a lot more than it would have hurt that parent. We would have suffered the consequences bitterness brings—not just in our personal lives, but possibly as a spillover in the relationships we cared about the most.

Hebrews 12:15 warns us, "See to it that no one falls short of the grace of God and that no bitter root grows up to cause trouble and defile many."

It certainly wasn't easy, but my wife and I chose to forgive this anonymous parent. Why? We wanted to obey God. We also wanted God to heal our hearts and for us to live in our freedom in Christ. After we forgave, it took awhile for our emotions to catch up, but they eventually did.

To clarify, we haven't forgotten what happened unjustly to Bekah. In fact, we may never forget. But we have forgiven, and our resentment is gone. And if we do remember and start feeling angry again, we realize this is from Satan. Our response is not to dwell on this offense, but to tell Jesus we know we have already forgiven that person.

Once you learn to truly forgive, you can repeat it every time you feel offended with any person in any situation. It's especially helpful as well as essential in marriages.

If You Wait to Feel Like Forgiving, You Will Never Forgive

Jack dragged his feet as he came into my office. Earlier, I had given him an assignment to forgive people who had offended him throughout his life.

"I don't feel like forgiving," Jack said with a solemn face. "I'd rather eat nails today than forgive all these people. I don't want to think about all those people and recall what they did to me."

"I could tell you were struggling by how you left marks on the carpet as you dragged your feet with every step, Jack," I said. We both laughed. "Seriously, though, nobody feels like forgiving the very first time they do it. It's something we do by faith, not by how we feel."

Jack thought for a minute and then said, "Okay. I will do this by faith even though I don't feel like doing it." He prayed out loud that day in my office, and when he finished he said, "Though I'm drained, I feel like a giant elephant has been lifted off my shoulders I didn't even know was there. I have such a deep peace, I can't fully describe it. But it's so real. It's what I've been searching for years to find. I had no idea that forgiving is what was missing. Now that it's over, it's one of the best things I've ever done!"

The relief and change in Jack's demeanor were apparent. If you, too, forgive, you can enjoy this same peace and will then be empowered in two areas. First, you will be equipped to forgive when someone offends you in the future. Second, you will not wait until you feel like forgiving. Jack was one of the fortunate ones who didn't let his feelings keep him from forgiving. Some never get there.

For instance, a man named Terry flew all the way from Europe to see me. Halfway through our counseling sessions, I taught him about forgiveness and sent him back to his hotel to prepare for our follow-up session the next day. The following morning, however, he called me to say, "I'm at the airport about to catch a plane back home."

"Terry, are you sure you want to do that? I discussed with you yesterday how much peace and healing you can experience. I wish you would change your mind."

"No, Mark. I'm going home. I think I've gotten as far as I want to get with the counseling. I'm done. Thanks for all you did for me."

Satan didn't want Terry to enter the freedom of forgiveness. Terry was deceived into thinking he couldn't go through with it and flew back home just as miserable as when he had arrived.

I tell Jack's story and Terry's story because Satan will also attempt to prevent you from forgiving other people. Your mind may scream at you that forgiveness is impossible.

Don't believe Satan's lies. You can forgive. God has forgiven you. I will show you how to forgive no matter how you feel. You are a forgiver in Christ. You also have in you the greatest Forgiver ever living to help you. Take that step of faith and forgive. You can do it by faith!

You Can Be Tortured by Unforgiveness

Let's look again at Jesus's discussion about forgiveness with Peter. Matthew 18:34–35 says, "His lord, moved with anger, handed him over to the torturers until he should repay all that was owed him. My heavenly Father will also do the same to you, if each of you does not forgive his brother from your heart" (NASB).

These verses are clear. Jesus is saying God will take back his forgiveness from anyone who doesn't forgive. In other words, they will go to hell! But let's remember something here. Jesus was speaking to people who were under the Old Covenant. That's how it worked. If you obeyed, God blessed you. If you didn't obey, God punished you.

Today we are under the New Covenant. In the New Covenant, God blesses us because of Jesus's obedience. If we don't forgive, because we are under this New Covenant of grace, God will not take away our forgiveness and we will not go to hell. Our motivation for forgiving is not fear, but love.

Ephesians 4:32 tells us to forgive *because* we have been forgiven in Christ, not to prevent God from removing our forgiveness. "Be kind and compassionate to one another, forgiving each other, just as in Christ God forgave you."

However, the consequences of unforgiveness will feel like hell in our personal lives. This is not God's punishment, but we will be tortured by our unforgiveness. Let's look at Ephesians 4:26–27: "In your anger do not sin: Do not let the sun go down while you are still angry, and do not give the devil a foothold."

God knows we are going to feel angry at times. When we do, we haven't necessarily sinned yet. It's how we handle that anger that determines if we sin. If we talk it out and work it out with the person who offended us, we will often avoid sinning. If we forgive quickly we will often avoid sinning. This is why we are told, "Do not let the sun go down while you are still angry." God wants us to deal with offense quickly. He doesn't want us to become bitter and sin. He knows how detrimental that will be to us and possibly to other people. He loves us and wants what is best for us.

If we don't deal with offense quickly, however, our unforgiveness gives the devil a foothold. In other words, this makes us vulnerable to Satan's attacks. This is where the torture in us often occurs. It's not punishment from God; it's the consequences of unforgiveness. In my counseling experience, I've observed five types of torture people experience when they don't forgive others:

1. Mental Torture

   Satan is allowed to feed our unforgiveness with further thoughts of anger. We then become increasingly obsessed by these thoughts of what they did and what we would like to do to get justice against them. That is where we want them to experience pain because of what they did. This alone is mental torture for most of us. It consumes our thoughts for long periods of time.

   Some believe unforgiveness can cause certain mental illnesses. That may be true, but it is certainly not the cause of all mental illnesses.

2. Emotional Torture

   Unforgiveness results in all kinds of other sins. Without forgiveness, these sins can be expressed through increasingly painful emotions, which grow into monsters that control us. Ephesians 4:31 describes these sins and the accompanying emotions: "Get rid of all bitterness, rage and anger, brawling and slander, along with every form of malice."

   It is also well known that unforgiveness can result in depression. We see in our counseling all the time that unresolved anger turned inward can cause depression. We also see that unresolved anger turned on others can inflict depression on them!

Please know clinical depression and anxiety are in most cases not related to unforgiveness. They are physical conditions where the body's brain chemistry is not functioning properly. In this case you need to see a doctor for medication, which God can use to help you.

3. Relational Torture

   People with unforgiveness most often are unable to have close relationships, and they often can't figure out why. It's because they have a wall up to protect themselves from further hurt. In other words, they are afraid of closeness. They also give off the vibe that they will not allow anyone in, and others sense it.

4. Physical Torture

   Human beings cannot internalize negative emotions week after week, month after month, and year after year without causing damage to their bodies. Unforgiveness is a poison that can bring great pain to us physically.

   Some believe people can develop specific physical maladies from unforgiveness, such as high blood pressure, arthritis, bulimia, anorexia, heart disease and cardiac arrest, stomach ulcers, back problems, headaches, chronic pain, and even cancer. But unforgiveness is not always behind these or other diseases and afflictions.

5. Spiritual Torture

   Long-term unforgiveness gives Satan the opportunity to oppress people. This is not demonic possession. (Demonic possession is not possible for a Christian.) However, oppression from Satan can still control a Christian in varying degrees.

   Christians who are oppressed often feel a heaviness, almost as if it is in the atmosphere around them. It's like a fog always there, such as the ever-present cloud of dirt surrounding Charlie Brown's friend Pig-Pen in *Peanuts*.

An oppressed Christian's mind and emotions can become so negative that he or she has difficulty functioning in daily life. New Covenant counseling can help close doors to oppression by taking a person through the forgiveness process.

Considering the various types of torture caused by unforgiveness, doesn't simply forgiving someone sound better? You have everything to gain by forgiving and nothing to lose! The benefits are multiplied many times over.

Forgiving is not only obedience to God; it's one of God's ways of loving you! However, you may be wondering how to forgive from your heart as Jesus told Peter.

How to Forgive from Your Heart

How do you know whom you really need to forgive? Some people might be obvious while others may not. The best way to discern this is to sit down in a quiet place with pen and paper. Then pray and ask the Holy Spirit to show you the people you need to forgive. God has a much better memory than you do and wants you to experience your freedom in Christ. As he begins to show you whom you need to forgive, write down these three things:

1. The name of the person who offended you. (If necessary, don't leave God off the list—or even yourself.)
2. What that person did to offend you. (List the actual thing the person did to you.)
3. How that made you feel then or even now. (You might feel angry, hurt, betrayed, bitter, resentful, or abused, but it's essential to express your emotions to forgive from your heart.)

This exercise may take awhile, even a few days. Once you've written everything down, keep it in a secure place since this is between you and God and no one else.

Then in a private place, select each person one by one and use the following prayer as a guide to forgive each individual:

Father, I'm coming to you now to forgive _____.
He/She did this to me: _____ and I feel

_____.

_____ doesn't deserve my forgiveness. But I didn't deserve your forgiveness either, and you forgave me for all my sins when I placed my faith in Jesus Christ as my Savior. I forgive because you tell me to forgive even as you completely forgave me in Christ. I also realize I am a forgiver through my identity in Christ. I choose to forgive _____ even though I don't feel like it. I release this person from what they owe me, which was/is _____.

I'm sorry for my sin(s) of anger/bitterness/revenge toward _____. I thank you that Jesus Christ died on the cross for this sin so that I am already forgiven. I choose to trust you and to believe that you can use this experience to reveal Jesus Christ in me in a deeper way. In his name, Amen.

You can pray this prayer for each person God showed you. Fill in the blanks with what you need to forgive every person on your list. Once done, destroy your list by burning it or deleting it!

A Prayer to Release God from Your Anger

Some Christians are also really angry with God. You may think he let you down or betrayed you. Yet it may be difficult to admit it because you believe you should not be angry with him. But if it's there, you need to face it.

What about forgiving God, though? How can we even remotely think we need to? He's perfect and cannot sin. He makes no mistakes. But we sure feel like he does at times, and that's what we need to deal with. He already knows we're angry with him, so we're not going to surprise him when we admit it.

Here is what I suggest. Instead of using the word *forgive*, use the word *release*. When we release God, we are acknowledging that we are angry with him, but in our hearts we are also releasing him from what it seems as though he owes us. It's for our benefit.

Twenty-five-year-old Alex came to me for counseling because he felt angry all the time. After a few sessions together, he finally realized he was angry with God for letting his dad die when Alex was ten years old.

After I taught Alex how to forgive biblically, he knew he needed to deal with his anger toward God. I led him through this prayer so he could release God and get rid of his anger:

Dear God, I realize I've felt angry toward you for letting my dad die when I was ten years old. I release you from letting my dad die. You don't owe me a dad who is alive today, though I miss him often.

I'm sorry I have lived in my sin of bitterness toward you. I thank you that Jesus Christ died on the cross for this sin so that I am already forgiven. I choose to trust you and to believe that you can use this to reveal Jesus Christ in me in a deeper way. In his name, Amen.

After praying this prayer, Alex left a freer man. His anger toward God was gone, and soon he began to experience a sense of intimacy with him he never thought possible.

If you have anger, hurt, or disappointment toward God, you can use this same prayer to release him. Replace Alex's struggle with your own struggle. Tell God exactly how you feel. He already knows, so it's okay for you to be honest and face it. If you're concerned about more than one issue with God, pray this prayer for each one.

A Prayer to Forgive Yourself

Surprisingly, the most difficult person to forgive can be ourselves, because we are often harder on ourselves than anyone else. We also don't think we deserve our own forgiveness. That can't be true, though. If it were, it would mean our standard for forgiveness is higher than God's.

Some Christians believe it's not biblical to forgive yourself. I agree it's not if you're trying to replace God's forgiveness with your own. But we can be assured that forgiving ourselves is biblical. We forgive ourselves because he has already forgiven us.

Remember Michael and Isabella at the beginning of this chapter? This may blow your mind, but the most difficult person for Michael to forgive was not his wife, who had committed adultery. Neither was it the man who had committed the adultery with her. The most difficult person for Michael to forgive was himself.

After our initial counseling session, I sent him home to pray and write down the names of all the people he needed to forgive and what they had done. He later returned with a ten-page list! When I asked to look over it, I noticed he was the person on his list who had done the most to offend him.

I encourage people to go through the forgiving process with me in my office. In Michael's case, it took three weeks of sessions for him to forgive everyone on his list. The very first thing he told me was, "Please don't ask me to forgive myself. I'm not ready to do that."

"That's fine," I said. "You can forgive other people." So he forgave many people, including Isabella.

When he returned the second week, I asked, "Michael, are you going to forgive yourself today?"

"No, I'm just not ready to do that."

"Okay. You can continue forgiving some of the others on your list."

When he walked in the third week, the first thing he said was, "I'm finally ready to forgive myself today." After I prayed for him, I told him to go ahead. He forgave himself for many things. I want to use Michael's prayer as a guide to show how you can forgive yourself.

Father, I come to you today to tell you I feel disappointed in myself. I feel like this because I have not been the spiritual leader in my home. I did not lead Isabella or our children spiritually. I have failed them, and I don't like what I've done.

I don't feel as though I deserve my own forgiveness, but I know that is not the truth. You forgave me for all my sins through the death of your Son, Jesus Christ, when I didn't deserve it. If you forgave me, I can forgive me. I also realize I'm a forgiver through my identity in Christ. I choose to forgive myself. I release myself from the debt of failing to lead my family spiritually.

I'm sorry I have lived in my sin of bitterness toward myself. I thank you that Jesus Christ died on the cross for this sin so that I am already forgiven. I choose to trust you. I believe you can use this to reveal Jesus Christ in me in a deeper way. In his name, Amen.

The Freedom of Forgiveness

Sometimes it can take awhile for our feelings to catch up with the healing from forgiving. But it will come. If Satan reminds you of what someone did to you, however, immediately go to Jesus in prayer. Tell him you know you've forgiven that person, and ask him to replace Satan's lie with the truth.

The big question is, When are you going to do it? Just knowing you need to forgive will not help you. To forgive you need to decide when you are going to do it. Is it right now? Is it tonight? Is it this weekend? Even if it takes more than one time to forgive everyone on your list, that's okay. However you do it, decide now when and where you are going to forgive.

God's New Covenant teaches us how to offer forgiveness to others and yourself, and it no longer needs to remain secret. You don't need to live in the darkness of anger, bitterness, and resentment. Forgive, and not only will you be glad you did, but other people around you will be blessed by your freedom in Christ!

10

Christians Can Be Controlled by Their Unknown Lies

Nicholas came to me for counseling, and here's how our conversation went in our first session.

"I just can't seem to relate to women, Mark," Nicholas said. "Sometimes I wonder if something is wrong with me. I'm a Christian, and I want to have good relationships. But now I'm worried I'll die a lonely old hermit. When I go out with a woman, I always seem to blow it. Something hurtful comes out of my mouth, or I say something critical. I try to apologize, but then it happens again. So she loses interest and it's over.

"My friends say I'm a great guy, but that I have low self-esteem. I know I get down on myself a lot. When no one else is around, I think to myself, *I'm so stupid. I'm weak. I can't get anything right.* But here's what doesn't make sense. I'm really good at my job. I've been promoted three times in five years, and my boss says

I'm about to get promoted again. How can I be great at work, yet so lousy with relationships and negative toward myself?"

"Nicholas, would you mind telling me what growing up was like for you?"

"Well, it was a painful part of my life. I'm a firstborn son, but my mom really wanted a girl. She acted like I was a burden and didn't want me around. Then when I was seven she had my sister, Elaine. I could tell she loved Elaine more than me. For example, Mom would buy my sister new clothes, but I only had used stuff to wear. And at Christmas, Mom would buy my sister lots of new toys, but I'd only get one present.

"Worse, if I disobeyed my mom, she'd lock me in my room for twenty-four hours. I wouldn't even get any food. But she never treated my sister like that when she was bad. Eventually, I couldn't take it and started running away when I was thirteen."

"That's horrible, Nicholas. No child should ever be treated that way—it should be considered a form of abuse. Where was your dad when all this was happening?"

"He would just go along with whatever she wanted. He wasn't very involved. Mom was in charge."

"Have you ever thought about what messages you heard about yourself resulting from the way your parents treated you?"

"Well, I guess my mom led me to believe I didn't belong in our family. I've also thought that maybe something was wrong with me, or she wouldn't have locked me in my room. I've never told anybody this, but I don't trust people—especially women. I believe they're always going to hurt me. And God doesn't seem to do anything to stop it. At least, that's been my experience."

"Could it be that you're programmed to believe you're defective?"

"Absolutely."

"That means you're being controlled by shame. Feeling shame isn't the same as feeling ashamed. It's the belief that something is wrong with who you are. It's called condemnation in Scripture, something God says in Romans 8:1 that he has freed Christians from. That verse says, 'There is now no condemnation for those who are in Christ Jesus' [NASB]. Could it also be that your parents and past relationships led you to think you have little worth and don't belong in relationships? If so, do you think God could offer a different way to view yourself?"

"I'm certainly open. I'm so tired of feeling this way."

I continued my conversation with Nicholas for several weeks. He was trying to answer a question many Christians ask: "How can I emotionally heal from past experiences and trauma?"

I've found that mental and emotional healing is not separate from spiritual growth; it's an essential part of spiritual growth. Mental and emotional healing replaces negative feelings with a sense of peace and well-being most of the time. To understand this connection, it would be good for us to look at another aspect of spiritual growth.

Spiritual growth is learning to live more dependent on Jesus in us to be our everything so we can live the abundant life God intended for each of us.

When Christians are counseled from a New Covenant perspective, they can begin to experience the reality that Jesus truly is the answer to their mental and emotional struggles. That is what Christians want to believe. They want to believe Jesus is the answer to their struggles, including their mental and emotional ones, but they rarely hear that. In over twenty years of counseling, I've seen that the more Christians learn to rely on Jesus to live in and through them, the more they experience mental and emotional healing. With that in mind, mental and emotional struggles are indicators that Jesus is being hindered from living in and through a person. This usually points to areas where the lies of the flesh of Christians are controlling them. I introduced the Bible's use of the word *flesh* in chapter 3, but we're going to unpack it further in this chapter as we learn how flesh is developed and howits subsequent patterns harm us.

Counseling based on the New Covenant helps Christians understand their flesh patterns so their mental and emotional pain can be healed by Jesus in them. Isaiah 61:1–2 points to this healing ministry of Jesus Christ when he came to earth:

> The Spirit of the Sovereign LORD is on me, because the LORD has anointed me to proclaim good news to the poor. He has sent me to bind up the brokenhearted, to proclaim freedom for the captives and release from darkness for the prisoners, to proclaim the year of the LORD's favor.

Jesus brings the good news of salvation to the poor. One of the meanings of salvation is to "make whole." The poor includes those in need spiritually, emotionally, mentally, or financially. Part of Jesus's ministry is to make people spiritually, mentally, and emotionally whole.

Jesus came to bind up the brokenhearted. This means he came to put your broken heart back together with his love. He frees people whose lives have been wrecked by their own sins or the sins others have committed against them.

Jesus came to free the captives. Many Christians are held captive by the lies they believe. Jesus frees us from those lies and replaces them with his truth.

Jesus came to provide release from darkness for prisoners. He came to release us from Satan's oppression. This oppression includes mental and emotional turmoil. It also includes people imprisoned by their habitual sins.

All this is still the ministry of Jesus today. Jesus is our answer for mental and emotional healing. His salvation includes this healing as one of the amazing blessings he wants for us. Though mental and emotional healing is not automatic, it's still something he wants us to experience.

How Does Hurt Happen?

Emotional pain is most often the result of sin—sins we experience from others, sins we commit, our incorrect perception of others' sins toward us, or living in a sinful, broken world. It can also be caused by mistakes people make, which are not sin but just mistakes.

However, the flesh causes our emotional pain, and each of our flesh patterns is formed by the input we get about how to meet our God-given needs.

We are all born with the God-given needs to feel secure, to feel competent, to feel accepted, to feel loved, and to feel esteemed. But because life can seem like scaling a mountain in search of fulfillment, I like to sum it all up with the acronym SCALE:

> Security
> Competency
> Acceptance
> Love
> Esteem

We can spend our entire lives trying to meet those needs through the flesh or we can let God meet those needs for us. When we're young children, we have no idea how to let God meet these, so we look to many other sources. We look first and foremost to our parents. God intends to live through a dad and a mom to express himself through them to meet the SCALE needs of children—to a certain degree. Yet parents often fail because they live according to their flesh, especially when they don't understand the New Covenant.

When that happens, children feel rejected and these needs go unmet. Rejection is an important message that can help form our flesh patterns. You can look for those times in your life when you felt rejected as a way of helping you discover any flesh patterns you've developed.

We Can Be Great Recorders but Bad Interpreters

In the first chapter of this book, I shared how my dad's criticism negatively shaped my view of God. Satan also used my father's sin to cause me to feel rejected. This formed my fleshly strategies for living life. I believe many other times Satan was the one who put the thought in my mind that I was inadequate. As a result I felt inadequate because feelings are a result of our thoughts. Satan wanted me to live from a flesh pattern of inadequacy based on lies.

Do you understand how my dad's sin caused my emotional pain? Do you see how it was an opening for Satan to tell me lies?

But let's change the story for illustration purposes. Let's say my dad just had a bad day at work and he was tired and hungry. He said I missed a spot when I mowed the lawn not because he was being critical but because he wanted to get into the house and eat dinner. My perception was wrong because I didn't realize how my dad felt or see the discouragement on his face.

When that happens, children can be great recorders of information but really bad interpreters of information. This means children sometimes come away from an event in life with the wrong perception. In that case, mental and emotional pain comes from the perceived sins of others.

Emotional pain can come from other sources too. It can be the result of consequences from our own sins, mistakes we make that are not sins, difficult circumstances, or traumatic events.

Not knowing who we are in Christ, we believe the lies Satan presents. I also believe Satan inserted another lie into my mind—as his solution to fix myself. This lie—*I must work hard to be the best so I can prove I'm adequate*—became one of the central lies that set the course for my life. Little did I know how much stress, emotional pain, and relational difficulties believing that lie would produce.

As adults, we are more conscious of when we are wronged. When another person's sin affects us, we are more outraged. Yet we respond to it just as a child does. We feel we've been knocked off a mountain we're scaling in search of security, competency, acceptance, love, and esteem. When we don't know how to find the source of these needs in Christ, we set ourselves up to be harmed by our own destructive patterns. That is one of the things I think Galatians 6:8 means when it says,

> Whoever sows to please their flesh, from the flesh will reap destruction.

For example, Katherine came in for counseling right after her first Christmas as a new bride. She believed her in-laws wanted to destroy her marriage to their son, all because her mother-in-law had wanted to help her cook Christmas dinner. She was stewing in deep resentment. She believed this was a clear message from her mother-in-law that she did not think she was a good enough wife for her son.

When I asked her if her in-laws had approved of their marriage, she said they had. She also said they had welcomed her into their lives and loved her from day one.

Puzzled by this, I probed for more about Katherine's upbringing. In doing so, the Lord worked in her to help Katherine discover that she had felt insecure much of her life around any women who tried to help her. This went back to her childhood when she misinterpreted her first-grade teacher's motive in asking her to come in early so she could tutor her on basic math. Katherine "heard" that she was inadequate, which made her feel insecure. From that point on she didn't want women to help her with anything.

Katherine's emotional pain was caused by her own misperception of her mother-in-law's motives for offering to help with Christmas dinner. Katherine believed a lie that needed to be exposed, a lie that started in her childhood and had become a flesh pattern in her. She was trying to protect herself from feeling inadequate around other women.

How to Identify Your Flesh Patterns

To heal from mental and emotional pain, we must understand the life strategies we adopt to compensate for the hurt we've experienced as a result of the wrong messages we have heard and believed about ourselves. We call these strategies "flesh patterns." But what is a flesh pattern? First, a flesh pattern is sin. Sin is often defined as missing the mark, but the Bible has a clearer way of defining it. Romans 14:23 says, "Everything that does not come from faith is sin."

While this verse related specifically to whether Christians could eat meat sacrificed to idols, the definition transcends the situation to give us a clear definition of sin. Sin is anything you or I do apart from depending on Jesus Christ. The flesh, then, is patterns of sins.

That is why the Bible describes the flesh as desiring to do the opposite of what the Holy Spirit in us wants to do. Galatians 5:17 makes this clear when it says, "The flesh desires what is contrary to the Spirit, and the Spirit what is contrary to the flesh."

Let's also remember what the flesh is not. The flesh is not the old self. Romans 6:6 and Galatians 2:20 both make very clear that the old self was crucified with Christ and has been replaced by the new self, our identity in Christ. When people interchange the old self and the flesh, Scripture is confusing. The old self is what makes someone a sinner in their identity. The flesh, however, is different, whether or not a person is a follower of Christ.

The flesh is not just sins we commit; it represents any strategy a person develops to cope with life apart from depending on Jesus Christ. Even as Christians, we all wrestle with trying to meet our needs for security, competence, acceptance, love, and esteem apart from God.

We are all born with flesh, yet the flesh is unique for each of us. Why? Because it is most often shaped by our childhood as well as our teen and adult lives.

I really like the way *The Message* describes and lists the flesh in Galatians 5:19-21:

> It is obvious what kind of life develops out of trying to get your own way all the time: repetitive, loveless, cheap sex; a stinking accumulation of mental and emotional garbage; frenzied and joyless grabs for happiness; trinket gods; magic-show religion; paranoid loneliness; cutthroat competition; all-consuming-yet-never-satisfied wants; a brutal temper; an impotence to love or be loved; divided homes and divided lives; small-minded and lopsided pursuits; the vicious habit of depersonalizing everyone into a rival; uncontrolled and uncontrollable addictions; ugly parodies of community. I could go on.

The flesh then is all the ways you've learned to cope to meet the deepest God-given needs of your heart apart from dependence on Christ. It's all the negative and positive strategies you now use to try to make your life work apart from Christ. Another way of saying it is this: the flesh is all the ways you've tried to give your life meaning apart from Christ.

Although a Christian can never be separated from God, the flesh is living "as if" we are separated from God even though we are united to him. Every time we rely on ourselves instead of our God, with whom we are united, we are living according to the flesh.

The flesh presents to us a false identity. It mixes together our wrong thinking, feelings, behaviors, and the opinions of others to create a false identity rooted in a self-centered focus on ourselves. It is completely contrary to our identity in Christ.

Some of our fleshly strategies may go away the moment we're saved. For example, I've seen people in counseling who were immediately freed from an addiction to alcohol when they became Christians. But they weren't freed from other issues—such as anger, resentment, and pride—that were causing problems in their relationships. Those were why they came to counseling.

All our flesh patterns don't disappear when we become Christians. Oh how I wish they did! But some people still struggle with sins they committed when they weren't Christians. For example, I've seen sincere Christians who were addicted to alcohol before their salvation still struggle with it.

The difference is that now they don't want to commit those sins, but they may not know how to stop.

Understanding Your Flesh Patterns

Every Christian has their own unique flesh patterns. No one has exactly the same strategies for living according to their flesh. However, you can usually put any flesh pattern into one of two categories: negative flesh or positive flesh.

This goes back to the Tree of the Knowledge of Good and Evil, which represents living life according to the flesh. While we often think of sin as all the bad (negative) things we do, this tree makes sure we also understand that sin also can be all the good (positive) things we do. It doesn't matter if it's negative or positive; if we are doing anything apart from dependence on Jesus Christ in us, it's sin! These sins can become negative or positive flesh patterns. I think this is what Jesus had in mind when he said, "Apart from me you can do nothing" (John 15:5).

When Christians have negative flesh patterns, they tend to have negative thoughts and feelings almost every day, which can lead to negative behaviors.

When Christians have positive flesh patterns, they think positive thoughts most days, and as a result feel positive. These people probably wake up feeling as though it's going to be a great day every day. They also tend to have positive behaviors.

Based on this, would you say you lean more toward "negative flesh" or "positive flesh"? Here's a simple exercise that might be helpful. Below you will see two lists of fleshly strategies. Put a check mark by any pattern of behavior you see in your life.

Let's start with negative flesh patterns, though this is not an exhaustive list.

Negative Flesh Patterns

- Abusing others
- Adultery
- Addiction to drugs
- Arguing disrespectfully
- Bitterness
- Committing murder
- Controlling people
- Dividing people (in a family or a church)
- Envy
- False guilt
- Fighting
- Getting drunk
- Gluttony
- Gossip
- Habitual anger
- Inadequacy-based living
- Inferiority-based living
- Jealousy
- Lying
- Performing for acceptance
- Practicing witchcraft
- Rage
- Rebellion

- Rejecting others
- Same-gender sex
- Sex between singles
- Sexual lust
- Shame-based living
- Stealing
- Viewing pornography
- Worry

The prodigal son in Luke 15:11–32 is representative of people with negative flesh patterns.

In contrast, positive flesh patterns may seem superior to negative patterns, yet they are just as destructive. You may have grown up in a loving and affirming family, even a Christian family. You may not feel a lot of emotional pain or struggle in your life. In fact, you may wake up feeling great every day.

If so, consider this: Did your parents teach you your identity is in Christ? If not, your self-image is still false even though it may be positive. Also, did your parents teach you to rely on Jesus Christ in you to be your primary way of coping with life? If not, you may be living dependent on your positive flesh, but it's still flesh. This will eventually catch up with you and cause emotional pain either in your life or for those you love. Put a check mark by any of the issues below you wrestle with as a positive flesh pattern, though this is also not an exhaustive list.

Positive Flesh Patterns

- Acting with superiority
- Arrogance
- Codependence (trying to make sure everyone is happy instead of loving them correctly)

- Exercise and nutrition for self-centered purposes
- Focusing on doing what is right and wrong, rather than what is loving
- Perfectionism to feel good about yourself
- Performing well for acceptance
- Philanthropy apart from depending on God
- Practicing "religion"
- Practicing legalism
- Practicing moralism
- Pride
- Self-reliance instead of reliance on Jesus
- Self-righteousness
- Serving God for the wrong reasons
- Spiritual disciplines for the wrong reasons (praying, reading your Bible, giving, and so on to prove to God, yourself, and/ or others that you are a good Christian)
- Too much television, social media, video games, or sports
- Trying to be a good Christian
- Trying to be a good person
- Trying to impress God, yourself, and/or others

Like the older brother in the prodigal son story Jesus told in Luke 15:11–32, Christians who struggle with positive flesh patterns tend to harbor these thoughts:

- *Why wouldn't God love me? I live a good Christian life.*
- *I'm a great person. Look at all I've done to help people.*

You may also feel some positive feelings of being lovable, acceptable, successful, superior, or even arrogant. These beliefs and feelings may show themselves as pride, always having to be right in an argument, self-righteousness, or the need to control.

Some Christians grow up with negative flesh but attempt to change themselves by trying to replace negative thinking with positive thinking. They use their performance to measure their improvement or lack thereof. When they perform well, they believe they are much better people and Christians. When they perform poorly, they believe they are inferior people and Christians. Their attempt to change has nothing to do with Jesus changing them.

On which list did you check the most behaviors? Add them up. Is your "flesh" more on the negative or positive side?

Here is some great news. Regardless of whether your flesh patterns are negative, positive, or some of both, God loves you too much to let them succeed indefinitely. He will let you run with them only for a while—until you begin to see they're not going to work.

You can try to overcome your flesh patterns through spiritual disciplines, more service to God, or an accountability partner. But you can't change your flesh. You can't improve your flesh. You can't stop your flesh. In other words, you can't fix your flesh with your flesh. One of the best parts of God's best-kept secret is that he offers his only alternative to wrestling with your flesh, which shows us why New Covenant Christianity is easier than we think.

God's Answer to the Flesh

The flesh, whether expressed in negative or positive patterns, works against relying upon Christ. So part of our maturing process is to let God expose these self-centered strategies. He reveals these issues by showing us three things:

1. Beliefs about ourselves based on our life experiences.
2. Feelings we express based on each belief.
3. Behaviors we exhibit to cope with the pressures of life.

In Nicholas's case, he grew up with a mother whose treatment sent a message that he was defective. Feeling rejected, Nicholas believed people—especially women—could not be trusted because they would betray him. He felt fearful of women, so naturally he developed a strategy to cope with this fear by preventing them from getting too close. That sabotaged his relationships.

We all develop similar strategies to meet our deepest needs. But when we live by strategies of the flesh, our minds are filled with lies. Romans 8:6 says, "The mind governed by the flesh is death, but the mind governed by the Spirit is life and peace."

The idea is that the thoughts that fill a person's mind are going to control their emotions and behaviors. A mind filled with lies will cause death. The word *death* in Romans 8:6 does not mean we will die; it means we'll experience emotional struggles and pain and other consequences as we try to meet our God-given needs as if we are separated from God.

In contrast, Romans 8:6 also says that when our minds are filled with God's truth, the results are life and peace. This is because Jesus is meeting our God-given needs. The flesh is the source of our mental and emotional struggles. Jesus is the source of our healing and stability.

As I shared these truths with Nicholas, he tearfully replied with a smile, "Mark, this is some of the best news I've ever heard. I can see why I've felt so confused about myself and my relationships. I'm ready to change. Show me how Jesus can meet the needs of my heart and heal the pain from my past."

Three Central Lies That Can Control Our Lives

I talked about lies earlier, but I want to help you discover the three extremely significant central lies that underlie all other lies. In other words, we have other lies we believe, but as I wrote earlier, they fan out from each of these central lies.

179

After years of counseling Christians, I've found every person is susceptible to falling for three central lies from Satan. They are each a hub around which our flesh and subsequently our pain is intertwined. Understanding them is key to living free from emotional pain.

The three central lies are: (1) your central lie about God; (2) your central lie about yourself; (3) your central lie about others. You can read about these three lies as they unfold in Genesis 3:1–10.

The central lies, along with other ones, often start in childhood. Satan inserts them into our little minds when we're young and impressionable, but we are unaware of it. As we grow up, Satan continues to repeat these lies by interpreting many life situations with them, which reinforces them. In other words, we can grow into adulthood and never realize for decades that we've been duped by Satan.

Your three specific central lies are discovered through interacting with God. You can be sure he will speak to you, usually by putting thoughts in your mind that possess the quality of peace. Jesus said in John 10:4 that we know his voice when he speaks to us.

You may have never taken the time to listen, though. Letting God expose Satan's lies is a great way to start the listening process. Go to your Father and ask him to reveal each of these three central lies in your life. Wait to see what he puts in your mind. If you receive no clear answer for one of them or all three, continue asking each day until each one becomes clear.

Here are the three kinds of central lies:

1. Your central lie about God

Juan, who had lost his brother at a young age, discovered his central lie about God was "God is unfair." He often felt bouts of anger and depression as well as anxiety. When God revealed this lie, Juan came to understand the truth that God is loving, not unfair. Juan's anger, depression, and anxiety were replaced with God's love and peace.

2. Your central lie about yourself

Marie discovered the central lie about herself was "I'm superior to everyone." This led to many of the positive flesh patterns listed earlier and caused a lot of problems for her at work and home since she always thought she was right. She believed she was in control rather than God. When God made this central lie clear to her, he replaced it with the truth that she is humble in Christ. Since then she has learned to rely on Christ for a balanced, accurate view of herself.

3. Your central lie about other people

I counseled a man named Gabriel who believed "Everyone will ultimately reject me." This lie caused him to become angry anytime someone made a critical remark toward him. God showed Gabriel that people will disappoint him, but that doesn't mean everyone will reject him. God spoke the truth to Gabriel that he is accepted in Christ. Slowly, Gabriel learned to open himself up to more relationships and take risks.

Like Juan, Maria, and Gabriel, when you live based on your own three central lies from Satan, you live according to your flesh, no matter how much you love God. To help you discover your three specific lies, let me share some prayers that can be helpful. Don't try to figure these out on your own, but pray instead and let God help you.

God, please show me my central lie about you. (You also need to pray God will show you your central lie about yourself. Then pray he will show you your central lie about others.)

As each central lie is revealed to you, you can then pray immediately:

God, what is the truth you want to show me that will replace this lie?

As each central lie and God's counteracting truth becomes clear, you can go on to this next prayer:

Father, I have sinned by believing the lie [name it] and have let it control my life. Thank you that Jesus died for that sin and that you have already forgiven me for it. Based on the finished work of Jesus, I ask you to break the power that this lie, [name it], has held over my life. I now thank you for the truth that you have shown me that [name the truth]. Whenever I'm tempted in the future to believe this lie again, please remind me of this truth. Amen.

There are some whose problem isn't lies but a physical issue. Those Christians may need medication for mental and emotional problems or other types of illnesses affecting their mental state. Thank God he has provided medications to treat these conditions. Some, but not all, are able to stop or decrease medications for mental and emotional issues under their doctor's care after they get counseling with us.

Let God's Love Reveal Your Central Lies

When someone understands the reality of God's love, it often reveals and heals them from the central lies from Satan they've believed. Here's an incredible testimonial from a woman named Shanika who experienced freedom in the midst of a damaged life:

Before coming to counseling, I was on the path of recovery from drugs and destructive relationships with men. I had received Christ at an early age, yet inside I felt empty, numb, and unworthy of God's

182

love—much less anyone else's. I didn't know how to deal with the pain, which is why I started doing drugs to escape the hurt and shame of believing the lie, "I'm not good enough."

I fell for the world's lie that I should try to love myself, and it worked for a short time. But there were still those days when I woke up feeling a black cloud of depression consuming me. I was overwhelmed with fear that if I did not deal with my anxious thoughts, I might lose all control.

The lies I believed also led me to purposefully sabotage relationships just to prevent someone else from taking steps to abandon me. Oh, what twisted thinking I had! There were nights that I begged God to take me home to be with him. I didn't want to kill myself, but I did not want to live anymore either.

After running out of options to solve the problem myself, I decided to seek counseling. The biggest thing I learned was that I'd been living my life according to fleshly coping strategies, which is apparently what most Christians do. I was living from lies instead of God's truth. These lies just led me to feel inadequate and ill-equipped as a Christian and as a person. In short, there was no total surrender of my life to Christ. The most beautiful truth that Jesus has revealed to me is that he truly loves me (little ole me), inside and out, and that in him, I am good enough.

Thanks to counseling based on God's truth, I can now say, "Hi, my name is Shanika, and I am deeply in love with Jesus my Savior, my best friend, and the lover of my soul." Life can still be hard and old feelings try to creep up. But knowing that Jesus loves me and lives through me gives me a reason to smile and face each day with a new perspective. Now when I look at my reflection in the mirror, I see Jesus. I don't see a disheartened and damaged woman anymore. She died with him on the cross and was resurrected with him to a new life. The best is yet to come!

God's truth provides the freedom from our flesh patterns. One aspect of the New Covenant best-kept secret is the reality that we don't need to look anywhere else to find freedom from the lies and strategies that control us. Jesus is the only answer we need.

11

Sinning Is Not Normal for Christians

"I just can't stop my excessive drinking—and I'm a pastor! My struggle with alcohol has dogged me for years. Each time I go to the bottle, I feel overwhelmed with guilt, condemnation, and shame. Some days I wonder if something is literally wrong with me. How can a Christian leader like me act like such a hypocrite?"

Those were the heartbreaking words spoken to me by Bob. He was the type of person most Christians think never has any problems. Yet Bob was in mental agony.

"No one knows about my drinking, not even my wife," Bob continued. "When I fail, I promise God I'll never do it again. But eventually the stress of my job kicks in and I'm defeated again. I hate it! I want to live free, but I don't know how."

Bob had been to seminary and knew the Bible inside and out. He'd tried quoting Scripture to himself, praying, and fasting, but none of that helped him conquer his habit. He'd also read several

Christian books on addiction and self-control. Yet the benefit was always short-lived.

"Mark, what am I missing? Is there any hope of real, lasting victory? Or do I just need to accept the fact that this is the best it gets? I really hope you can show me an answer."

Do you feel about your own struggle with sinful habits the way Bob felt about his? Do you resign yourself to believing this is the best things will ever get? Do you accept your struggles and soldier on?

Every Christian struggles with temptation and habits. Many end up feeling hopeless against destructive thoughts and behaviors. But you're not alone in your battle against tempting desires. God has the answer we all need to overcome sin. Yet his approach to victory is like a little-known truth hidden from most Christians. In this chapter I want to share how victory doesn't occur by trying harder or getting an accountability partner.

Sinning Is Abnormal for a Christian

One of the most important things God wants you to know is that sinning is no longer normal for a Christian. It's abnormal. Why? Because you are a righteous child of God who is now like your Father. Being born into your Father's family means it is more normal for you to live a righteous life than a sinful life. That doesn't mean you will never sin. You will. But remember, we are no longer sinners; we are righteous.

We see the truth that sinning is abnormal for Christians in 1 John 3:9: "No one who is born of God will continue to sin, because God's seed remains in them; they cannot go on sinning, because they have been born of God."

When you understand sinning is not normal for a Christian, a lot of writings in the Bible make more sense. All the exhortations to live a life of holy and righteous obedience are encouragements to live like who we are in Christ. There's a difference between obeying to become more holy and righteous and obeying because we are already holy and righteous in Christ.

Here is a different perspective on how to define sin in your life. If obedience is living like who you are in Christ, then sinning is living the opposite of who you are in Christ. But you may be asking yourself, *Then why do I sin if I really am righteous in the core of my being? Why do I still get defeated by some of the same sins over and over? I truly do not want to sin, but I keep doing it.*

Don't worry. You are in good company. Paul is considered by many people to be one of the greatest Christians who ever lived. Yet he went through a time in his life when he felt defeated too. This is why he wrote in Romans 7:15, "I do not understand what I do. For what I want to do I do not do, but what I hate I do." Just like you and me, Paul didn't want to sin, because he was a righteous child of God. But he could not stop until God showed him the answer.

Maybe you have committed the same sin so many times you have begun to wonder if you are even a Christian. For instance, maybe, like Bob, you've tried to stop drinking. Maybe you've tried to stop abusing drugs. Maybe you've tried to stop fantasizing about a sexual relationship with someone. The same could be said about trying to stop gossiping, worrying, being jealous, staying angry, and more.

A genuine Christian hates sinning because it's the opposite of who she or he really is. But people who aren't Christians usually don't want to stop sinning unless the consequences cause some kind of discomfort—like losing their job or marriage. Other times they may quit bad behavior if someone gives them an ultimatum. It's important to make the distinction between a true believer and someone pretending to know God.

For example, a young man named Quan came to see me during his summer break because his parents had forced him to. They had threatened to stop paying for his college expenses because of his excessive partying.

Over the next few months, Quan began to trust me and seemed to look forward to his appointments. He finally revealed that he was not only partying, but having sex with his girlfriend and stealing surfboards from a nearby rental store to sell—all with no remorse. The Holy Spirit prompted me one day to ask him some questions.

"Quan, when you get drunk, do you feel sorry about it?"

"No, not really. Why would I?"

"When you have sex with your girlfriend, do you feel sorry about it?"

"Why should I? Everyone else is having sex."

"When you steal those surfboards, do you feel sorry about it?"

"No, all my friends steal now and again. It's not hurting those rental places."

"Do you want to stop doing any of these things?"

"No, I want to keep doing them. I actually enjoy it."

"Quan, I care about you enough to tell you the truth. Though you've been in church your entire life, I'm not sure you are a Christian, and here is why. It's not that a Christian can't do any of those things I asked you about. They can. But when they do them, they don't like it. They feel godly sorrow. And most of all, they don't want to keep doing them. Do you think you are a Christian?"

"No, based on what you just said, I don't. And I don't want to be one right now, either."

"Then there isn't much I can say to help you. So our time may be done, but you are welcome to come back anytime."

Surprisingly, a few months later, Quan showed up again. As soon as he sat down, he said, "I'm back because I can't take it anymore. My parents stopped paying for college, I ran out of money, and my girlfriend is upset with me. I realize I need God. Can you help me?"

We talked about what it means to become a Christian through faith in Jesus Christ. Afterward, Quan prayed and became a Christian. The following week, he returned and told me that he'd had sex with his girlfriend again. This time, however, he said, "I hated the way I felt afterward. I don't want to do that anymore. Can you help me stop?"

I said, "Yes, I can show you how Jesus can help you stop."

Do you see the difference? After Quan became a Christian, it wasn't about right and wrong. It wasn't about arbitrary rules, not getting caught, or skirting consequences. As a true child of God, sinning was no longer normal. But like a lot of Christians, he just didn't know how to stop. I was able to show him how Jesus could help him. Quan eventually experienced victory over these habits and grew to be a strong influence for Christ.

Temptation Does Not Originate within You

As a Christian, do you know temptation itself is not sin? Even Jesus was tempted, but he never sinned. If you give in to temptation, then you have sinned. But do you also know temptation never comes directly from you? It can't once you are joined with Christ.

As we have already discussed, according to 2 Corinthians 5:17, a Christian is a "new creation," meaning our deepest and true self. Since this true self is holy, we cannot initiate sinful thoughts of any kind. It's impossible. Your identity in Christ can initiate only thoughts that are good, wholesome, holy, and righteous.

For example, think about any thoughts you have of inadequacy. Do you ever have thoughts that make you feel insecure, worthless, or inferior to other people? Guess what. None of those thoughts come from you. Evil thoughts cannot originate within you, because only one true self is within you. It's the new self, created in Christ when you believed in him by faith.

Remember, you are not a sinner in your core. As a Christian, you are a saint in your core. That prevents any sinful thoughts from originating from who you really are in Christ.

So you're probably wondering, *Why do I think sinful thoughts as a Christian?* Here's why. It appears as though sinful thoughts come from Satan and his demonic world. That's why in Ephesians 6:11 we're told, "Put on the full armor of God, so that you can take your stand against the devil's schemes."

This tells us Satan and his demonic world strategize against us as Christians, trying to defeat us. One of his best strategies is to put sinful thoughts directly into our minds. Have you ever been praying and had a sinful thought come from nowhere? Sure. We all have.

I know we've touched briefly on this, but I'd really like to dig deeper here, because we often believe erroneously that tempting thoughts originate from us. I want to pull back the curtain so you can understand the real truth behind those thoughts.

Here's Satan's masterful trick: *He can insert thoughts in your mind that sound just like you.* He knows your human weaknesses and your strategies, where you tend to live independent from God. As a result, he will attempt to get you to live from the flesh in those same areas again anytime he can. And he will mimic your own internal voice to tempt you.

For instance, if you are a female from New York, Satan's tempting or hurtful thoughts will sound like a female in your mind with your New York accent. If you are a male from Georgia, Satan's thoughts will sound like a male with your Georgian accent. Satan can even mimic your fast or slow speech.

The thoughts may be in first person and use the word *I* or *me*. They may also be in the second person and use the word *you*. Can you understand why we believe tempting thoughts come from us? They sound just like us talking to ourselves in our heads.

When I teach this to Christians, I often see a visible sigh of relief. It's a liberating feeling to understand that sinful thoughts don't come from us. Why? As long as you believe sinful thoughts are your own, you will conclude that you're a dirty, rotten sinner, and a horrible Christian. Naturally, you will define yourself as a terrible person because of the awful thoughts you think.

However, when you realize sinful thoughts don't originate from you, it brings a sense of peace as you embrace another benefit of knowing who you are in Christ.

If sinful thoughts don't originate from you, does this mean you can completely overcome temptation just by knowing Satan's tactic? No, but it's a starting place in this sense: when tempting thoughts come into your mind, you can say, *I know these sinful thoughts aren't coming from me.*

Along with temptation, Satan places negative thoughts in general into our minds throughout the day. We can reject those thoughts and walk in truth, or we can accept his thoughts and be misled.

I talked with a woman named Beverly who grew up with an alcoholic father who never spent time with her. When she was about ten, her dad became a Christian. He started spending all his time serving at their church instead of getting drunk. As wonderful as that sounds, he still never spent time with Beverly. But everyone at church thought her dad was great, and Beverly felt guilty when she felt resentment toward him.

When Beverly told me her story, I asked if she ever dealt with feeling insecure or unimportant. She immediately said, "Yes. I feel both of those all the time. How did you know?" I told her it was because she had already told me that by describing her relationship with her father.

Beverly went on to tell me how negative thoughts bombarded her almost every day. She said she spent her entire life trying to prove she was special, but she couldn't shake those negative feelings.

Some kids fight back in this type of situation and try to force a parent to change. Some kids realize their parent has a problem, not them. Other kids just give up and turn their attention to pleasing other people. Some kids, like Beverly, try to prove they're special to their parents.

Her feelings of inadequacy drove Beverly to try to be the best at everything—music, academics, dating, and then later even Christianity. She was always trying to prove to herself that she was somebody special. She believed if she could prove she was the best, she would be special.

Today Beverly knows she is special because of who God made her to be in Christ. Yet Satan is no dummy. Sometimes when Beverly fails at something, such as with a project at work, Satan takes advantage of that situation and puts old, negative thoughts in her head that sound just like her to try to get her to agree with him instead of agreeing with God. Sometimes Satan succeeds before she catches his trick, but not always. Since she now knows she has died to sin, to Satan, and to this world (Rom. 6:7; Col. 2:20; Gal. 6:14), she is much more aware of Satan's attempts. She sees them quicker and more often than she used to. When she does, she knows to go to Jesus and pray,

Jesus, I know because of my identity in you I am not an unimportant, sinful person, even though I may have failed. I believe I am a child of God, who is chosen in Christ and special to you. Take care of these thoughts from Satan as I agree with what you say about me, not him. Amen.

In what ways do you believe you aren't special? Where do you believe you don't measure up? Will you accept by faith today that sinful thoughts are not coming from you? If so, you will gain a tremendous advantage in overcoming temptation when it occurs.

Don't Say I Shouldn't Do This

Let's apply these truths to one of the most challenging temptations in our society today—pornography. Because of the internet, no one has to look for this problem. It will find you, even if you have special filters on your computer (which I do recommend).

Here's a conversation about pornography I had with one of my three sons when he was a teenager. I'd put together a father-son weekend. We had lots of fun together during the day and talked about serious issues in the evenings. I started our conversation by asking my son a qualifying question:

"Son, I know we've talked about this issue before, but I want to check in with you to see how you're doing with pornography. No matter what you tell me, I am going to love you and accept you. So please be honest."

"Well, Dad, to be honest, I'm not doing very well. I'm fine when you or Mom are at home. But when you both leave the house, I really struggle and usually lose the battle to look at porn online."

I knew it was embarrassing for my son to reveal his struggle, so I said, "Let me remind you again that I love you and accept you. Tell me what you do or think when the temptation occurs."

"Well, I tell myself I shouldn't do it because you wouldn't like it."

"I appreciate that. But does that approach help you overcome it?"

"No, not really."

"And it won't. Tell me what else you do."

"I tell myself I'm a Christian, and I shouldn't do something like this."

"Does that help you?" I asked.

"A little, but not for long."

"Neither of those approaches is going to help you, because you are 'placing yourself under the law' in an attempt to overcome the temptation. The two laws are 'I shouldn't do this because of my dad and mom' and 'I shouldn't do this because I'm a Christian.' There is no power in any kind of law to overcome temptation.

"Here's a grace-based approach. When tempted, remember that thought is not coming from you, because you are a saint in

Christ. And because you already understand the rest of the New Covenant, you can pray something like this:

Jesus, because I'm not under the law but under grace, I know I'm free to look at pornography. You will love and accept me even if I do. But I don't want to look at it because I know that in my identity in Christ, I'm not a pornographic person. I'm a righteous and holy child of God. To look at pornography is not consistent with my identity in you. I know this activity is not good for me. It is not for my benefit. It will hurt me. Please live through me to handle this temptation. I can't overcome it on my own, but I know you can.

"If praying this prayer doesn't seem to stop the temptation, it could mean you're dealing with a stubborn habit or are stuck in a prolonged pattern of Satan's lies. In that case, take the authority you have in Christ and tell Satan to leave you alone because you belong to Jesus. Do it out loud and say something like this:

Satan, in the name of the Lord Jesus Christ, in whom I sit at the right hand of the Father today, I command you to leave me alone right now. I belong to Jesus Christ, who lives in me. I'm not a pornographic person but a holy and righteous child of God. Be gone from me, in Jesus Christ's name.

"Do you think what I have shared is going to help?" I asked.

"Yes, Dad. I really do. I didn't realize rules aren't really helpful with stopping my thoughts and choices. I was putting myself under the law when I tried to fight temptation on my own. That just makes the problem worse. I now know how to ask God to resist temptation through me and believe that he still loves me and accepts me even if I fail."

"Great. I'll check with you in a few weeks to see how you are doing."

When I asked him about it a couple of weeks later, he said, "I'm doing great, Dad! I really know what to do when tempted to look at pornography now. I go to Jesus and overcome it by his power."

The Superior Sin-Stopping Option to Willpower

When you're tempted, do you try to overcome your particular issue by putting yourself under the law along with your willpower? When tempted, do you ever tell yourself something like this?

- *"I'm a Christian. I shouldn't do this."*
- *"What would my Christian friends think if I did this?"*
- *"I'm not going to do this, no matter what."*
- *"This is my last time."*
- *"I'll promise God I'm not going to do this again."*

All these admonishments are simply law-based methods that will never work. The law works only one way—to stir up sin. The Bible tells us,

> When we were in the realm of the flesh, the sinful passions aroused by the law were at work in us, so that we bore fruit for death. (Rom. 7:5)

> The sting of death is sin, and the power of sin is the law. (1 Cor. 15:56)

Whether or not someone is a Christian, sin uses the law as leverage to defeat him or her. Satan uses our willpower or self-imposed laws to get our focus off Jesus and onto ourselves. That will never work. However, when we stop trying to fight temptation on our own and focus on Jesus's grace and power, we can identify temptation as a destructive lie and walk free in the truth. Romans 6:14 tells us God's grace is the only way to overcome temptation:

> Sin shall no longer be your master, because you are not under the law, but under grace.

If you reverse this Scripture, you will see that anytime we try to conquer sin through a rule or a law, it will defeat us. The verse would read like this: "Sin will remain your master when you live under law instead of under grace."

Grace is God's only way to truly win the battles we all face with sin. And remember, grace is a Person. Grace is Jesus Christ. That's why 1 John 4:4 tells us, "Greater is He who is in you than he who is in the world" (NASB).

You can give up on trying to win over sin through the law and willpower. It will never work. Instead, you can rely on Jesus Christ in you. He is always greater than any temptation to sin Satan can put in your mind. First Corinthians 15:57 tells us we already have victory before we are tempted when it says, "But thanks be to God! He gives us the victory through our Lord Jesus Christ."

I'd like to encourage you to use the same prayers I suggested to my son. Simply insert the name of the sin you are tempted to commit.

As Christians, it's a huge relief to realize that sinning isn't normal for us. Sure, it's normal for a sinner to sin, because that is who he or she is in Adam. Christians can still sin, but it's not normal, because they are saints in Christ.

That is why, according to the New Covenant in God's Word, it's normal for you to live like a saint. Embrace the power God offers through grace to overcome sin in your life!

12

The Secular and Spiritual Are the Same for Christians

"I don't know how to say this, but I just don't feel important to God. My whole life has been spent as a wife and a mom who has raised daughters who moved far away. I've never done anything great for God. I've never had time to get deeply involved in ministry. And now that I'm an empty nester, I don't know the purpose for my life. Sometimes I wonder if God even thinks I'm worthy to be on his team."

These were the frustrations expressed by Wen. Yet her comments reflect similar concerns felt by thousands of Christian men and women. The problem revolves around the belief that God is most satisfied with Christians when we perform spiritually focused activities.

In chapter 6, we discussed how Christians were never created to follow rules. But there's a lingering confusion about separating behavior that is spiritual from behavior that is secular. And Satan can trick us into putting a premium on so-called "spiritual" activities that drive our sense of worth and belonging in God's family.

In our counseling session, Wen's comments reflected this misunderstanding. I said,

"So raising your girls was an important part of fulfilling your purpose. But what if God doesn't put our behavior into spiritual or secular categories? What if everything a Christian does is considered spiritual?"

"I've never heard that before," Wen said. "Aren't we supposed to focus on the fruit of the Spirit, always loving others, or something like that?"

"Yes, the fruit of the Spirit provides wonderful expressions of grace God wants us to enjoy. But God expresses his grace through us in many different ways. Let me put it like this. Have you ever gravitated toward certain activities over and over?"

"Well, I used to help out at our church's children's ministry, and I always enjoyed creating visual aids and painting props for the children to see. I loved doing that, but it didn't seem very spiritual. I was just painting."

"When you were younger, did you enjoy artistic activities?" I asked.

"Yes, I was always painting then. But my parents discouraged me from doing it too much. I was told to just study and focus on schoolwork. That hurt me, because I still wanted to paint. So I did it in secret and hid my paintings where no one could find them. But I also felt guilty about doing it. Once I got married and had kids, I just stopped painting. It felt like a waste of time, especially since I didn't think I was very good at it."

"Wen, I can't help but wonder if this is one of those talents God gave you as part of your divine design. Ephesians 2:10 tells us about our divine design as Christians when it says, 'We are God's masterpiece. He has created us anew in Christ Jesus, so we can do the good things he planned for us long ago' [NLT].

"To be God's masterpiece means you are his divine design. This means he gives every person their unique identity in Christ and a unique combination of talents, spiritual gifts, passions, and desires. He wants to use those things to serve and bless other people. The more Christians experience true freedom in Christ, the more they're liberated to live from their divine design. Your desire to paint may actually be coming from God. The more we understand that he doesn't divide the spiritual from the secular, the more his desires become clear to us."

Wen had always defined her desire to paint as a secular, unspiritual activity. To be a good Christian, she assumed, she needed to be subdued and focus primarily on things like Bible study. But as we talked she realized if Jesus Christ wanted to paint through her, then it was a spiritual activity—even if it was just for fun. As she made this discovery, I watched her smile with a new sense of joy.

Afterward Wen started to paint freely and even built an art studio in her home. Her talent for painting blossomed in ways she never could have imagined. She was "living the dream"—God's dream for her life that she never understood before.

Today, several of her paintings are displayed in local art galleries! More importantly, Wen realizes that being spiritual isn't based on conducting certain religious activities. God is glorified when she lives according to the divine design he places within her.

Everything a Christian Does Is Spiritual

Like Wen, the more you understand your freedom in Christ, the more you will realize life is no longer divided into secular and spiritual. For example, many Christians may believe their jobs are secular, but their service in church is spiritual. Cheering for a favorite sports team is secular, but singing praises to God is spiritual. Listening to any genre of music is secular, unless it is Christian music, which is then spiritual.

God enjoys living in you, so he enjoys the things you enjoy, such as watching your favorite movie, hiking, listening to music, reading books, or playing sports. Of course, he also enjoys living in and through you to study the Bible, to pray, to witness, to worship, and to serve. When God is living through you in any activity, it is spiritual. It's even worship and glorifies him. First Corinthians 10:31 tells us, "Whether, then, you eat or drink or whatever you do, do all to the glory of God" (NASB).

This is especially interesting, because the context of this verse is about the freedom strong Christians have in contrast to weak Christians. In fact, earlier in 1 Corinthians 10:23, Paul writes, "All things are lawful, but not all things are profitable. All things are lawful, but not all things edify" (NASB). Paul is obviously not approving sinful behavior. Jesus never leaves us, but he's hindered from living through us when the flesh is controlling us. When he is not living through us, the flesh is expressing itself through us at that time. Nonetheless, Paul is saying that, otherwise, because of God's grace, we are free to enjoy all of life.

Also, the word *secular* is not the same thing as the word *worldly*. To live worldly means to live sinfully. First John 2:16 is clear about what worldliness is: "Everything in the world—the lust of the flesh, the lust of the eyes, and the pride of life—comes not from the Father but from the world."

The lust of the flesh includes sex apart from marriage, drunkenness, abusing drugs, and gluttony. The lust of the eyes is a lack of contentment as displayed by always wanting to own the newest thing so you can try to feel happy. The pride of life is the arrogance of believing that you and not God are the center and source of your life. When Jesus Christ is expressing himself through us, the Holy Spirit will lead us away from a worldly life.

With this in mind, you may be wondering how you'll know if something is sinful when you're relying on Christ to live through you. That is a great question, which I believe understanding worldliness helps answer quite a bit. But you can rest assured that the Holy Spirit is going to let you know when you are about to sin or when you are sinning.

For example, the Holy Spirit will give you a lack of peace in your spirit about TV shows, music, movies, or video games that aren't consistent with God's character. When any of these activities or programs glamorize sin or show sin as normal, you will know deep inside that this is not what he wants you to do.

The last three chapters in Ephesians explain what our lifestyle looks like when we live consistent with God's character. That's why Ephesians 4:1 tells us "to live a life worthy of the calling you have received." Ephesians 5:1–2 expands on this idea when it says, "Follow God's example, therefore, as dearly loved children and walk in the way of love, just as Christ loved us and gave himself up for us as a fragrant offering and sacrifice to God."

God will never lead you to live a worldly life. Otherwise, all activities in life are spiritual when Jesus is living through you. He will lead you to live a holy life. A holy life is not living by a list of dos and don'ts. It's not about secular versus spiritual activities. A holy life is a life lived from God's love flowing through you. A life of love will always glorify God.

All of life is holy when Jesus is living through you. All of life is worship when Jesus is living through you. All of life glorifies God when Jesus is living through you.

If you've allowed a legalistic, religious mind-set to separate your behavior into secular versus spiritual categories, abandon that thinking right now. Take a moment to pray this prayer:

Dear Jesus, I realize that up until now I've divided life into secular and spiritual because of my legalistic, religious mind-set. I don't want to do that any longer. I want to live a life of freedom under your grace. Starting right now, I ask you to remind me that when you're living through me, everything

I do is spiritual, everything I do is holy, everything is worship, and everything except sin glorifies God. Thank you for revealing this truth as another liberating expression of the abundant life I have under your grace in Jesus Christ. Amen.

God Speaks to Christians outside of the Bible

Christians also incorrectly separate the secular from the spiritual because of another mistaken belief that God only speaks through the Bible. Sure, he mostly speaks to us as we read it, study it, memorize it, and hear teaching from it. But God also speaks in other ways outside of Scripture. When he does, it will always be in a manner that aligns with Scripture.

Years ago I counseled a pastor named David. David was a tremendous student of the Bible, but he struggled with anger toward himself and the church staff around him. He tended to be overly critical and push people away. In addition, David believed God stopped speaking to people outside of Scripture after the Bible was written.

As David and I talked during one of our sessions, he had no idea that God was about to turn his world upside down. I asked him to go home, find a place where he could be alone to pray, and ask God one simple question: "What do you think of me?"

When David returned the next week, I asked him to share what he thought God said to him. As he tried to speak, he began to choke up. David said, "I sensed God speak to me, 'You aren't the hot-headed, impatient bad guy you've always thought you were. In my eyes, you are a good son.'" He was confident that this message was from God, because he had formerly labeled himself a "bad Christian" because of his anger issues. This was actually the beginning of David experiencing freedom from those anger issues.

One of the biggest blessings of being a Christian is the ability to hear directly from God. John 10:3–5 says,

He who enters by the door is a shepherd of the sheep. To him the doorkeeper opens, and the sheep hear his voice, and he calls his own sheep by name and leads them out. When he puts forth all his own, he goes ahead of them, and the sheep follow him because they know his voice. A stranger they simply will not follow, but will flee from him, because they do not know the voice of strangers. (NASB)

In these verses, Jesus was telling a group of strict law-keeping Jewish leaders, the Pharisees, that they could not hear his voice. The reason was because they did not believe in him as their Savior.

For Christians, these verses say we can hear his voice. We are like sheep who can distinguish the voice of their shepherd. In the same way, hearing Jesus's voice starts with our salvation, but also continues afterward. Also notice that it does not say he speaks only to special Christians. It says every sheep—meaning every Christian—can hear his voice.

That doesn't mean he speaks to us with an audible voice. But it does mean he speaks to us. His voice is heard in our spirit through thoughts and impressions. That would make sense since we are united with him, wouldn't it? First Corinthians 6:17 says, "The one who joins himself to the Lord is one spirit with Him" (NASB).

How does God speak outside of the Bible? Consider if you've ever had any of the following occurrences happen.

1. Have you ever had a sudden urge to pray for someone who came to mind for no apparent reason?
2. Have you ever had the sense that you needed to call someone but you didn't know why?
3. Have you ever had a thought with such a special quality and specificity that you knew it wasn't coming from you?
4. Have you ever made a decision and then realized you didn't have peace about it, even though your mind convinced you the decision was logical?

5. Have you ever had a Scripture verse or song come to mind when you were praying?

6. Have you ever seen a picture come into your mind when you were praying for a situation or for someone?

7. Have you ever had a dream while sleeping that you just knew was God speaking to you?

Here is what you can understand about God's voice: though he mainly speaks to us through the Bible, he may also use other aspects of our daily lives to direct our paths, including movies, mental pictures, music, other people, and so on. That's because the secular and the spiritual are the same to him. He recently spoke to me so powerfully during a movie scene, I could hardly stop crying.

Take time to listen for his voice often. He will speak to you more than you could ever imagine.

You Are God's Will

As we seek to discover God's will for our lives, not only can we confuse the secular and the spiritual, but we can miss what is right in front of us. Often, Christians think God's will is mysterious and he hides it from us. But that's not the case. God's will is woven into our divine design so we can choose his will as he leads us into it. Relying on Jesus Christ to live through us every day is God's first and foremost plan for our lives. As we live this way, God's more specific will becomes more clear. In addition, we can sometimes miss what God is doing in our hearts or spurn the way he personally designed us.

Because of these issues, I want to provide some important questions for you to ask yourself. They are designed to give another perspective on understanding God's will for your life.

Let's start with looking at your passions. God plants desires within us that often turn out to be his will, whether a full-time job

or a part-time involvement. Use these questions to help identify
the passions that get you most excited.

1. If money wasn't an issue, what would you like to do with
   your life?
   I don't mean moving to Hawaii and going to the beach every
   day! It might be an activity you're already doing. Or it might
   be something you've always been drawn to but haven't ac-
   knowledged until now. It might even be something you currently do as a hobby.

2. What makes you feel really alive?
   Identify what causes you to light up when you talk about it
   or get involved with it. Remember, it can be anything, not
   just something that sounds spiritual to other Christians. It
   can also be helpful to ask someone close to you if they see
   the same thing you identify. Focus on identifying the passion
   God has given to you.

3. What specific topics or activities repeatedly draw your
   attention?
   The issues or actions that repeatedly capture our focus can
   also point to God's purpose for us. Sometimes we can do
   those things full-time, but it may be that we can do them
   part-time along with our profession.

4. What spiritual gifts have you experienced that give you
   great joy?
   Spiritual gifts are simply the unique ways Jesus lives through
   you to minister to other people. You can often recognize them
   because of ministry activities you enjoy doing that bless other
   people, whether formally or informally. If you are unsure
   about your gifts, trying different kinds of ministry can make
   them clear. Taking a spiritual gifts test at your local church
   or online can also be helpful.

Christians Can Do Whatever They Want

When God gave you a new heart, he gave you the desire to do whatever you want. This new heart, which is your identity in Christ, also desires more than anything else to do what he wants, which is essentially a grace-based, godly life. But God also works his desires through us as a process over time. I believe that's what Psalm 37:4 means for each of us when it says, "Delight yourself in the LORD; and He will give you the desires of your heart" (NASB).

Delighting yourself in the Lord is simply enjoying him as he lives in and through you. As you do, that is how he places his desires and dreams in your heart so they become your desires and dreams. These are not random. They are what God created you to do, which will bless people and fulfill you. We see that God doesn't free us just for our own fulfillment. He frees us so he can love, serve, and bless others through our lives. Second Corinthians 1:3–4 explains this clearly: "Praise be to the God and Father of our Lord Jesus Christ, the Father of compassion and the God of all comfort, who comforts us in all our troubles, so that we can comfort those in any trouble with the comfort we ourselves receive from God." You've heard, "You can do anything you want." The truth is you can do anything God created you to do.

For example, when I look back over my life, God had to move me from my desires and dreams to his desires and dreams. It was a progression I didn't even realize he was doing. Allow me to walk you through my journey to show the loving way God works. He led me on an amazing path to now be the founder and president of Grace Life International, a Christian counseling, teaching, and training ministry based in Charlotte, North Carolina.

I believe God placed the spiritual gift of leadership in me on the day I became a Christian at age nine. But this gift didn't start to reveal itself until my early teens. I remember thinking to myself as a teenager, *I'm well liked. I can have influence in people's lives.*

I found myself interested in teaching people the Bible during high school. To be honest, I had no idea what I was doing, but it was my first glimpse at the spiritual gift of teaching within me. It happened when I invited some of my friends over to my house and tried to share the meaning of the Bible. To this day, I still appreciate the way they patiently listened to my ramblings.

When I was in college, I would often pray, "Jesus, what is your will for my life? I'm willing to do anything you want me to do. I'm willing to go anywhere you want me to go. Please make your will clear to me."

For many months afterward, nothing seemed to happen. But God was answering that prayer more than I understood. As I look back, I can see the early beginnings of counseling traits God had placed in me. I always experienced a deep joy when I listened to my friends and taught them the Bible in helpful ways. I still struggled to fully perceive my spiritual gifts, talents, and God's will in college, but I could tell when I really enjoyed something.

A few years later, after finishing seminary, I got a job on staff at a large church as a youth pastor. But I felt a desire well up within me to be a lead pastor and preach one day. Occasionally I got the opportunity to preach, which stoked the fire within even more. Even better, I met my wonderful wife, Ellen, during this time. She was definitely God's will for my life!

As time progressed in my thirties, however, I couldn't shake the desire to be a lead pastor. So I ended up starting a church. Though I didn't understand my identity in Christ at the time, I gravitated toward counseling people in the congregation. After a few years, the church fell apart and I hit rock bottom. Surprisingly, that wasn't the end of God's path. It was actually a new beginning, because that painful time led me to discover the New Covenant and the depth of God's grace. In that turmoil, God revealed himself even more.

With renewed vigor to share biblical truths with others, I joined a ministry that used the New Covenant message in their counseling, teaching, and training materials. It was a perfect fit, and I loved it. Yet the leadership gift within me rose up again. So I talked with the ministry leadership, and we agreed that God was directing me to start a similar ministry in Charlotte, North Carolina. We named the organization Grace Life International, which is where I'm still excited to work today.

Because a fear of failing again loomed large in my mind, however, I moved to Charlotte with some trepidation. So before my wife, small children, and I made the move from Atlanta to Charlotte, I prayed this prayer in earnest: "Lord, you know when I attempted to start a church I failed miserably. So as I prepare to start this new ministry, I feel afraid again. But I am also sure of something else. If you don't live through me to lead this ministry, it will fail too. But if you will live through me, this ministry will be whatever you want it to be."

The day I started Grace Life, I was fulfilling another part of God's dream and desire for my life. From the time I became a Christian at age nine, he had been patiently and lovingly preparing me for this journey. That doesn't mean there haven't been failures along the way. But I've seen God's hand at work throughout the process. I never could have imagined he would take Grace Life from a starting staff of four people to over forty counselors! I'm still amazed at the way God has grown the organization to a national level with international partners.

Best of all, my staff and I have watched God change thousands of lives over the past twenty years. I've seen thousands of marriages saved, thousands of individuals healed from tremendous mental and emotional pain, thousands more freed from destructive habits, thousands enter into deeper intimacy with God, and thousands serve God more effectively.

As you read my story, you may also wonder about God's plan for your life. My experience has shown this truth: discovering God's will is dependent upon Jesus living through what you are doing today. You may or may not be at the last stop on your journey, but it's the stop where you are parked for now. You can trust God in the place where you find yourself. But walk with a mind-set open to him taking you to the next place that's part of his plan.

I can assure you that God has a specific plan for your life. Some of it you may already know. Some of it you may not yet know. Examine your desires, review your past, and ask God to show you the good works he created you to do. His plan may include a hobby you enjoy, ministry opportunities, or even the job you currently have. He will make it clear.

Part of God's best-kept secret is that there's no difference between the secular and spiritual. It's all just one amazing life in Christ. And the more you allow Jesus to live in and through you, the freer you become to live as the divine design he created you to be. In other words, you become freer to be yourself!

This world is in need of you, the unique person God planned you to be long before time began. He wants to live in and through the special you he designed to bless this hurting, needy world during your time in human history.

I'm reminded of an encouraging quote that captures this truth in a marvelous way. It's from Howard Thurman, an influential African American author, theologian, philosopher, educator, and civil rights leader who mentored leaders such as Martin Luther King Jr.

"Don't ask yourself what the world needs. Ask yourself what makes you come alive and go do it, because what the world needs is people who have come alive."[1]

1. "About Us," Howard Thurman Center for Common Ground, accessed June 7, 2017, www.bu.edu/thurman/about/history.

Conclusion

CHRISTIANS HAVE GOD'S BEST-KEPT SECRET WITHIN

Several years ago, my wife and I were blessed by friends who generously offered to pay for us to take a restful vacation as a way to support my counseling and teaching work. The timing of their offer was perfect. We needed a break from our busy schedules since the ministry was growing tremendously.

At my friend's encouragement, I suggested Hawaii as the location. It felt surreal when a couple of days later he emailed back confirming the idea. "We would love to pay for you and your wife to take a vacation in Hawaii!" he wrote. I never dreamed of receiving such a lavish gift. The whole trip was paid for before we ever got there.

After arriving in Hawaii, my wife and I snorkeled with beautiful fish of every color imaginable. We walked the stunning white beaches and sunbathed in the warm Hawaiian sun. But our most amazing experience was hiking a scenic mountain ridge created by a volcano hundreds of years ago.

As we climbed this particular trail, it was a perfect day with clear blue skies, puffy white clouds, and green, lush scenery. The trail was so steep in places that we had to use ropes someone had placed to help pull ourselves up the steep incline. However, nothing could prepare us for what we saw as the trail neared the top of the mountain.

The path became very narrow. A fall down the right side would be a long drop into a ravine with trees everywhere. If we fell down the left side, we would tumble over and over until we finally hit the bare bottom of the mountain. But as we braved ahead to the top, the view from that summit called Mount Olympus was absolutely breathtaking, and we could see almost the entire island below us.

In one direction, we could see the famous North Shore, known for its powerful waves that propel the adventurous souls who love surfing. The eastern side of the island offered a view of Bellows Beach, one of the most amazing beaches in the world. To the south, we could see the city of Honolulu, outlined by the beautiful and famous Waikiki Beach, where we were staying, and the old volcano, Diamond Head, an unmistakable landmark.

My wife and I stood together in awe of what we were experiencing. We turned to each other and agreed that it was worth the risk we had endured to arrive at such an incredible scene. We felt as though we were on the top of Paradise. We wondered how many people on the island had lived there for their entire lives but never known the full beauty of their own area.

I believe the Christian life is similar to that experience we felt vacationing in Hawaii.

First, our vacation was fully paid for by someone else. Likewise, Jesus fully paid for our salvation. Let me remind you of all he paid for on our behalf:

- God now lives in us just as he once did in Adam. God is on his throne, but he is also living inside of us so we can be loved by Father, Son, and Holy Spirit. We can live every day confident that we are loved. This is what makes us fully human.

- God is not expecting us to live by a religious checklist. He wants us to live from the inside out because we have Jesus in us as our life, our strength, our wisdom, our righteousness, and so much more. He is our only true Source for living. No person, achievement, or possession can adequately compete with him.

- We were resurrected with Christ and given a new identity. For example, if anyone ever asks who you are, respond without hesitation, "I am not who I was when I was born. I am not what I do. Through faith in Jesus Christ, I am a child of God and a saint, even if I sometimes still sin."

- We are as righteous as God in our new identity in Christ. We don't live perfectly and we never will. But we will always be unconditionally accepted by God because he made us perfectly righteous.

- Our new identity in Christ assures us we do not have two selves warring against each other. The old self was crucified with Christ and is gone forever. We now have only one new self, which was resurrected with Christ. Your new self is perfect, holy, and good in Christ.

- Jesus died so we could be forgiven before we ever sin. We need never worry whether God will be angry with us. We can run to him instead of away from him when we mess up.

- We died to the Ten Commandments and all religious rule-keeping with Christ on the cross. We no longer need any of those laws to show us how to live. Instead, we live by the Holy Spirit in us. We can live like who we are in Christ since the law has been written on our hearts.

- God can use our suffering to strengthen us. He does this by freeing us from our dependence on the bankruptcy of our flesh as he reveals Christ in us more and more.

- God gives us the grace to completely forgive the people in our lives who do not deserve it, just as he forgave us when we didn't deserve it. As we do, we enjoy freedom from resentment and bitterness we may not realize we are carrying.

- When we sin, the problem is usually related to lies from Satan, which he uses to program our flesh. Satan does this to cause us mental and emotional pain. But Jesus can then heal us mentally and emotionally as we believe and live from his truth and replace the lies.

- Sinning is no longer normal for us as Christians. Jesus Christ is greater in us than Satan and our sins. As a result, we can experience genuine freedom from longstanding habits.

- There is no division between secular and spiritual when Jesus is living through us. And no matter what we're doing, we can hear God's voice more than we thought possible. His divine design points us to actions and desires we were created for before time even began.

Second, just as the trail my wife and I hiked in Hawaii became narrow, the path of Christianity is narrow. When Jesus spoke about salvation in Matthew 7:14, he said, "The gate is small and the way is narrow that leads to life, and there are few who find it" (NASB).

Jesus Christ is the only gate by which a person can enter salvation. There is only one way to God and that is through Jesus. If you have never truly become a Christian, there is no better time than right now to do so. Pray this simple prayer:

Dear God, I realize I've been separated from you for my entire life. As a result, I've made many mistakes and committed a lot of sins in my attempt to find meaning in life apart from Jesus Christ. I now place my faith in Jesus Christ alone, believing he died to forgive me for all my sins. I also believe he rose from the grave to come live inside of me and make me truly alive for the first time in my life. I'm glad I no longer have to search for my identity. I believe I'm becoming a child of God even as I pray this prayer, whether or not I feel it. I believe Jesus Christ is now my Savior, Lord, and Life. Thank you for loving me more than I could ever understand. Amen.

If you are a Christian, maybe you read this book and realized you've been misguided about who God really is. Maybe you believed misconceptions about the Christian life. Maybe you discovered your life revolves more around trying harder and legalistic rules than you assumed. That's why I say the Christian life is a narrow path. We can experience great stress by falling off the trail into a religious form of Christianity that isn't really Christianity at all.

In contrast, you can also be greatly damaged by falling off the other side of the path through seeking pleasure and satisfaction in worldly pursuits, rather than seeking God's truth. Maybe the initial fun you experienced is wearing off. Maybe you've started to realize how those choices just lead to emptiness.

The narrow road of Christianity is neither religious legalism nor self-focused worldliness. The narrow way for a Christian is walking the path of grace. This path represents Jesus Christ himself, who wants to live in you and completely love you. Then he wants to live through you to live out Christianity each day in ways only he can accomplish to bless other people. Our response is simply to rely upon him for it all.

I wrote this book to offer you a new beginning in your relationship with God. But I'm not talking about promising God you will do better, try harder, be more committed, or rededicate yourself to him. It's a new beginning where you leave all that stuff behind and abandon yourself completely to Jesus Christ as your only real hope for living life as God intended.

Just as I did on the narrow trail I hiked in Hawaii, you will have both difficult times and joyful times as you walk through life. But as you walk in the truth, you will see the beauty of God and his amazing grace. Enjoy marveling at the incredible view of who God really is and the authentic Christianity he offers through Jesus Christ. Take that step today by praying this prayer:

Dear God, I realize I have been misguided in my quest to live the Christian life, to find my identity, and to enjoy you. I give up on relying on myself. I accept that I'm already forgiven for all my sins—past, present, and future. I give up on all my fleshly effort to be a good Christian. I give up on any kind of rule-based Christianity I've tried to live. I now place my reliance on you, Jesus, who lives in me.

I believe you are my only true Source of love and acceptance. I believe you are my only true Source to live the Christian life through me in the power of the Holy Spirit. Remind me often of these truths. May your life in me increasingly free and heal me as you live through me. As that happens, may you bless other people through my life. I pray this in Jesus's name, Amen.

My desire is that you live free forever because now you know the New Covenant, which fully explains God's best-kept secret. Though life always has its ups and downs, Christianity is easier than you ever could have imagined—since it's all up to Jesus Christ to live his life through us!

They will know God's secret, which is Christ himself.
He is the key that opens all the hidden treasures
of God's wisdom and knowledge.
Colossians 2:2–3 GNT

Mark Maulding is leader and founder of Grace Life International, one of the largest Christian counseling and teaching ministries in America. He is also a speaker, writer, mentor, counselor, and leadership coach. He is married to one of the most fun and funniest people he knows—his wife, Ellen. They have three boys and one special girl with Down syndrome, who all recently finished college.

Through years of personal failure, Mark knows firsthand the agony and heartache of believing in a twisted Christianity, causing a false view of God. He's now on the other side, having personally experienced the transformative power of understanding who God truly is and the purpose for which he created us. This understanding impassioned Mark to leave the pastorate and found Grace Life International in 1995. This is a growing, dynamic ministry with regional, national, and international influence through biblical, grace-centered counseling, conferences, training, and preaching. It has grown from four to forty staff and is reaching people all over the world through its online ministry.

Mark has spoken to thousands of people in churches of many sizes and denominations. He communicates passionately and warmly to help Christ followers live in the freedom they have always hoped for but have been unable to find. As a former pastor, he communicates with compassion but boldness, encouraging the church to consider the Christianity it preaches. As a result of his ministry, thousands have been transformed, including the typical person in church and the pastor in the pulpit.

Connect with

Relevant. Intelligent. Engaging.

Sign up for announcements about
new and upcoming titles at

www.bakerbooks.com/signup

 ReadBakerBooks

 ReadBakerBooks